The Assassination of Abraham Lincoln

The Funeral Car

Excerpts from newspapers and other sources

From the files of the
Lincoln Financial Foundation Collection

Objects from the Lincoln Funeral Car
Held by the Union Pacific Museum, Omaha, Nebraska

Desk

Funeral Car model

Objects from the Lincoln Funeral Car
Held by the Union Pacific Museum, Omaha, Nebraska

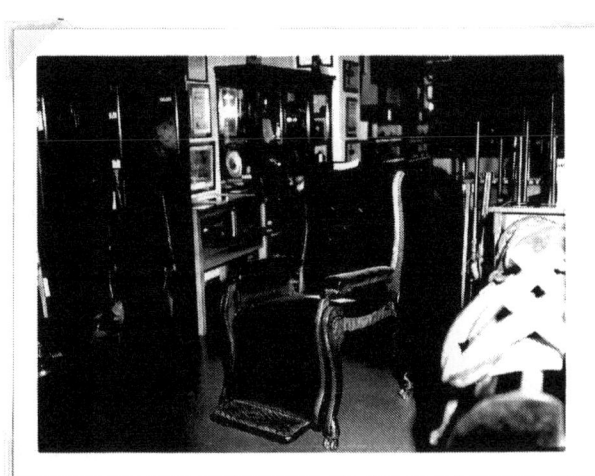

Reclining chair

Mahogany framed mirror

Objects from the Lincoln Funeral Car
Held by the Union Pacific Museum, Omaha, Nebraska

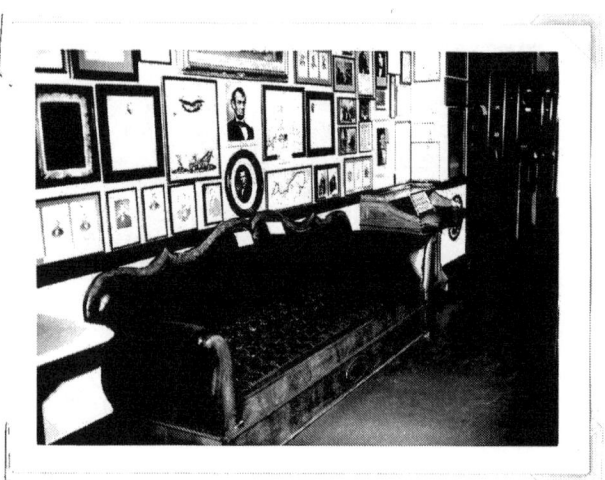

Long couch & desk

**Objects from the Lincoln Funeral Car
Held by the Union Pacific Museum, Omaha, Nebraska**

Silver Service Set

Bookcase and Couch

THE PRESIDENT'S FUNERAL CAR, ON A STEAM LIGHTER, APPROACHING NEW YORK FROM JERSEY CITY, APRIL 25, 1865.

VIEW OF THE FUNERAL CAR CONTAINING THE REMAINS OF PRESIDENT LINCOLN.

Leslie's Illustrated 1865

The Funeral
Car as it was ready
to leave for the ~~county~~
out to Springfield

W 1768
War Dept.
Apl. 12" 1866
L. 89

Directs the QMGenl
to vacate and set
aside the sale of the
Funeral car that
conveyed the remains
of Mr Lincoln to
Springfield, and all
disposition in regard
to it, taking measures
to have it safely
preserved until
further orders.

Sold Alexander U.S.
to Baulu R.R & co. for
a director car & 650 —
the return directed to show
[...] & procure car
Decision Bk 5, page 44
Recd QMG.O. own.
Apl. 12" 1866
W. D. Bk T.

See telegram to Genl Robinson
Alexandria Va. Apl 12"66

Washington D.C.
April 12. 1866

Maj. Genl M. C. Meigs
   Qr. Mr. Genl.
      Dear Sir:

Yours of this date informing me that the Secretary of War has disapproved the sale of the Saloon Car purchased by me, and asking me for information as to the purchase and intended use of this car is received and in reply I have to say.—

I purchased the car at what purported to be a public sale, supposing that Col. Robinson was authorised by the Secretary of War to make the sale. I bought it for Col. H. S. McComb, of Wilmington, Delaware, who is a Director in the Union Pacific Rail Road Company, who informed me that he wanted it for that Company.— The fiercest Bidder for it was a person who wanted

M 672
H. S. McComb
Washington D.C.

Apr 13 1866

Submits statement in relation to purchase of the "President's Car," &c by N. H. Larned for the Union Pacific R. Road.

Respectfully referred to the Secretary of War.

To keep this car will require a building to be erected for it, and a keeper or watchman retained. Relic hunters depredate upon it whenever they get the opportunity, as upon the curtains of the East room. The car was used not above as a funeral car. It had been used before the death of the President and has been used since. It sold for a fair price to a National Railroad Co. which proposes to use it as a director's car. The confirmation of the sale is recommended.

Rufus Ingalls
Quartermaster Genl.
Bvt. Maj. Genl. U.S.A.

Q. M. Gl. Office
April 13th 1866

Approved
Edwin M. Stanton
Sec. of War

Quartermaster General's Office,
Washington, D.C., Apl 13 1866.

Maj. Genl Meigs
 Q M Genl, U.S.A.

Sir; The passenger coach known as the President's Car, sold at auction at Alexandria on the 11th inst., was bought for me for the Union Pacific Rail Road Compy. Mr Ward or Lamon bid at my request for this reason that a Mr Williams who was also a bidder had announced it as his intention of buying it for the purpose of putting it on exhibition

Copy from The National Archives   Record Group No. 92

I inferred from this that if I bid on behalf of our Rail Road Compy Williams would run it up to an exorbitant price - and greater than if bid for by an individual - hence my request for Lamon to become nominally the purchaser - The price it sold for is it's full value - & as our work is a National enterprise - we thought it fitting that we should be the possessors of this Car - Truly H.S. McComb
Director U.P.R.R.Co

LINCOLN'S CAR.

DISMANTLED AND DECAYING IN OMAHA RAILROAD YARDS.

An Historic Relic That Was Made to Suit the Ideas of the Martyr President.

In an obscure corner of the yards of the Union Pacific car shops in Omaha, in a dilapidated and abandoned condition, stands a truly historic relic known as the "Lincoln car." Its sides are cracked and weather-beaten, and the glass in its windows and the brass railings on its platforms are long ago gone. All the compartments and sumptuous interior furnishings and decorations have been removed, and it stands like a barren, decaying bulk of its once proud self. From its former prominent association with President Lincoln, both during the later years of his life and then after his death, it would seem, says the Chicago "Tribune," the car deserves a better fate than to rot in neglect and obscurity. This car was built specially for Mr. Lincoln in the United States military car shops at Alexandria, Va., in 1864, by B. F. Lamason, master car builder, and was certainly one of the handsomest private railroad coaches in its day. It was used by the President repeatedly in his visits to the Army of the Potomac down in Virginia, and also to New York and Philadelphia.

The Lincoln car is forty-two feet long by eight and one-half feet wide, and during the time Mr. Lincoln used it was divided in three compartments. It was entered by a door in the corner, which opened into a narrow passageway extending the entire length of the car along one side. From this passageway doors opened into each of the three private rooms. The room in one end of the car was considerably larger than the others, and was furnished with a large sofa and reclining chairs. The small rooms were also provided with sofa and chairs, although somewhat inferior to those in the large room. This larger compartment constituted President Lincoln's office and study, and is where he entertained his guests and transacted business with officials of the Government and generals of the army. The sofa is a combination affair and was made of unusual length to accommodate the elongated form of the President. It was used as a sofa or lounge during the day and at night could be adjusted into a double bed of two berths—upper and lower —like berths in a sleeping car.

The car was considered in that day a triumph of the car builder's art. The walls of each of the compartments were padded with rich, corded crimson silk upholstery, reaching half way to the ceiling, and the frieze of the President's room was decorated with painted panels of the coats-of-arms of the different States of the Union. The car was ironclad, armor being set in between the inner and outer walls, rendering it bullet proof. This added considerably to its weight, so much so that the builders thought it necessary to mount it on four four-wheeled trucks.

Just after the close of the war the Government put a great amount of its railway material that had been used in the prosecution of the war into the hands of an auction firm in Cincinnati, and among it was the Lincoln car. Sidney Dillon, who was then at the head of Union Pacific affairs, was directly responsible for its purchase. For a long time after its arrival in Omaha the car was a great curiosity both on account of its connection with the martyred President and also for the reason that it was then considered the finest railway coach that had ever been constructed, and many thousands of people visited the car shops for the purpose of seeing it.

Late in 1892 a company of men from New York sent an agent to Omaha with a view of negotiating a purchase of the car, intending to exhibit it at the World's Fair. Satisfactory terms with the Union Pacific people could not be made, however, and the project was abandoned. The agent desired to have proof of the authenticity of the car from the railway officials, and Mr. I. H. Congdon, for many years master mechanic of the Union Pacific Railway, in a lengthy letter on the subject to Mr. E. L. Lomax, general passenger agent of the road, said:

"The famous car was brought to Omaha in 1866, and was purchased for the Union Pacific by T. C. Durant. Sidney Dillon manifested great interest in the car in the early days of the road. I was in charge of the locomotive department of the Great Western Railroad of Illinois, at Springfield, during the war, and was there at the time President Lincoln's remains were brought there. The car had been used as the funeral car, and stood in the railroad yards during the time that Lincoln's body lay in state in the Capitol building, and we had an opportunity of examining it closely. I remember identifying it as the same car when it came here in 1866. When first brought to Omaha it was used as a private car by the directors, but on account of its extreme weight and the manner in which it was mounted, it rode so poorly that they soon abandoned it. I have been over the road with Mr. Dillon in the Lincoln car, and heard him speak of it as being the one that the President used during the war, and in which his remains were brought to Springfield. Mr. S. H. Clark, now president of the Union Pacific, stated to me a good many years ago that Mr. Dillon desired some of the furniture of the car taken out and sent to New York, and I saw that his request was carried out.

"The car was built as nearly as possible to suit Mr. Lincoln's idea, and was so peculiar in construction as to give it individual characteristics."

After the death of Dillon and Durant the car was sent out on the mountain division of the Union Pacific, and was used in the desecrating capacity of dining-car for a construction gang. Unless the directors of the Trans-Mississippi Exposition or some showman or historic relic collector rescues it from its present obscurity the old car that carried one of the world's greatest characters during the latter end of his life and then, after death, to his burial will soon pass into disintegration.

LINCOLN'S COACH IN IOWA.

COLUMBUS JUNCTION.—The old coach in which Abraham Lincoln rode to the White House when he was inaugurated President, was transferred through this city where it remained on the side track for a few hours on a flat car en route to Kansas City where it is to be on exhibition. Many people visited it. One of Columbus Junction's pretty girls climbed into the coach and sat down in the seat occupied by Lincoln and had her smiling face caught by a camera. 5.23.51a

President Lincoln's Private Car.
Special Dispatch to the Globe-Democrat. 1893

OMAHA, NEB., May 14.—There stood on a side track under the Eleventh street viaduct last night an interesting relic of old-time railroading. It was the private car in which the martyred President, Abraham Lincoln, traveled about the country back in the 60s. It is a striking contrast to the palace on wheels of to-day. Running along the top of the car are the words, "Colorado Central Railroad," while beneath the window is painted the inscription, "work train," but so worn with age as to be almost indistinguishable. The car was brought in from North Platte yesterday, where it has been for years. It has been used as a boarding car for section men. It was built at Alexandria, Va., about thirty-five years ago. A narrow aisle originally ran along one side, with doors opening into the various compartments. It was taken to the Union Pacific shops this morning, where it will undergo a thorough overhauling and be put in the same condition as when President Lincoln occupied it. It will then be taken to Chicago for exhibition at the World's Fair.

A Valuable Relic.

The railroad car which Lincoln used whenever he went to the front during the later military operation in Virginia, and which bore his body to Springfield, Illinois, after his assassination, now remains a battered relic, in the yards of the Union Pacific railway at North Platte, Nebraska. The car was built expressly for the president at the United States military car shops at Alexandria, Virginia, in 1864, and since Lincoln's death it has had a varied career. It was used by the higher officials of the Union Pacific as their private car, and a special building was put up at Omaha to house it while not in service. Next it was permanently side tracked and used by the Union Pacific division superintendents to live in, and after a time it was converted into an ordinary day coach for passenger service. Now its usefulness is outgrown and it is experiencing the fate of an antiquated warship. 11.1.92

TO RESTORE LINCOLN CAR.

Historic Railroad Coach to Be Preserved in Omaha. 1500

Special Dispatch to The Inter Ocean.

OMAHA, Neb., Feb. 17.—The Lincoln car, built at the opening of the war, is to be given lodgment by the city of Omaha in a public building, if plans of Omaha colored people do not miscarry. For many years this curious piece of railroad equipment has been occupying a vacant lot at the Union Pacific yards, with other cast-off rolling stock.

The company bought the car shortly after the Lincoln funeral and used it in the far West as a pay car, it being especially desirable for this purpose, as it had half-inch boiler plate within its side, concealed by upholstering and mahogany. These plates were placed there as a precaution to prevent President Lincoln being shot while at the front, where he frequently went in this armored car. The Union Pacific found it desirable as a pay car because of danger of outlaw attacks. The car was the finest thing known to railroading in those days, but today it stands aside as the worst lot of rubbish imaginable.

The negroes of Omaha propose to have the council appropriate money to secure the car, have it restored as nearly as possible to its appearance when President Lincoln used it, and place it in a public building in the city, as a curiosity. Dr. M. O. Ricketts, a well-known colored physician, is behind the plan, and the negroes want the sole honor of the movement. Mayor Moores is a civil-war veteran, and looks upon the plan, with favor. The Union Pacific has not indicated what it will accept for the car, but the opinion is expressed that it will be donated to the city. The car has a number of bullet holes and shell marks in it.

Lincoln's Funeral Car.

Car 04, which is now used for outfitting purposes by the Union Pacific, has a remarkable record. It was once the property of the Pennsylvania railroad. At the time the people throughout the world were shocked because the news was flashed along the wires that Abraham Lincoln, then president of the United States, had been assassinated by John Wilkes Booth.

A few days later preparations were made for the removal of the remains of the martyr from Washington to Springfield, Ill. This coach, 04, was selected as the funeral car. After the remains had been laid to rest at the early home of the honored dead the Union Pacific company purchased the car as a memento of the lamented chief. At present the car is on the western section of the Union Pacific, where it recalls only to those who are well posted the hallowed memories which cluster about its walls.—Omaha Bee, June 7, 1885.

J WRIGHT

Funeral CAR

"LINCOLN CAR" DRAPED

Vehicle Which Bore His Body Placed on View at Omaha.

Omaha, Neb., Feb. 12.—Lincoln's birthday was celebrated by the Union Pacific Railroad by closing the entire headquarters for the day. President Lincoln's administration was especially identified with the building of the overland route, and the day was observed as much as possible over the system.

The "Lincoln Car," which stands dismantled at the old shops, was draped appropriately and people were given an opportunity to view it. In this car the body of the martyred President was carried from Washington to Springfield, Ill.

CONGER

FUHFRAL

THE LINCOLN CAR. A HISTORICAL RELIC.

This is the private car in which Abraham Lincoln used to ride when he was president. By contrasting it with some of the wheeled palaces which are furnished for the use of our chief executive today you get an idea of the progress we have made in this direction in less than half a century. The rebuilding of the shops of the Union Pacific railway at Omaha has brought to light this relic of wartimes, around which cling the memories of the martyr president. In 1864 the government built the car to be used by the president. It was most made use of in his visits to the Army of the Potomac. The car was built at the United States military carshops at Alexandria, Va. It is 42 feet long and 8½ feet wide and is divided into three compartments. It is ironclad, armor being set in between the inner and outer walls, rendering it bullet proof. The car was used to convey the remains of Mr. Lincoln for interment at Springfield, Ill. At the close of the war the government auctioned off a great deal of its railway material, and the Lincoln car was sold to Sidney Dillon, the president of the Union Pacific, and T. C. Durant, who removed it to Omaha. A shed was built for the car, and a man was engaged to watch and care for it. The intervening years have left their marks on the old relic.

Reporter a/r 26 1902

Brunier Neg. #31-602

UNION PACIFIC RAILROAD PHOTOGRAPH

This photo may be released for
publication on use of credit lines
"Union Pacific Railroad Photo"

FUNERAL CAR.

B&O News: Aug 7, '03

FAMOUS LINCOLN CAR HAS BEEN SOLD.

Was Ironclad for Protection of the War President--Genuine Curiosity.

OMAHA, Neb., Aug. 7.—The Union Pacific has sold the Lincoln car, which has been the property of the road for the last 37 years, and it will be placed on exhibition on The Pike in St. Louis next year. For years the car has stood on the tracks near the Union Pacific shops, and it has attracted scarcely passing notice of Omaha people except when it was on view at the Trans-Mississippi exhibition. It was also exhibited at Chicago in 1893.

The car was built at the military car shops in Alexandria, Va., in 1864. It was ironclad, armor plate being set between the inner and outer walls to make it armor proof. After the car was built the President used it practically altogether, and his remains were taken to Springfield for burial in it. In 1866 it became the property of the Union Pacific, and has only changed hands within the last week.

LINCOLN CAR.

Of all the interesting exhibits at the World's Fair, there is none that has created more general attention or is viewed with a greater reverence and affection than the old Historic "Lincoln Car" since its arrival and installation in the Lincoln Museum, World's Fair grounds. None of the visitors at the museum who see this sacred relic go away without gazing at the old coach for some time with affectionate interest, and few look at it save with uncovered heads.

Although the car now is in a delapidated condition, plainly showing that it has been abandoned to the cold storms of winter and the sun's hot rays of summer for too many years, it is still the car used by President Lincoln and his cabinet during the war and later carried his remains to Springfield, Ill., interment. Time has made sad changes both within and without. From a beautifully decorated exterior its sides are cracked and weather beaten. Inside the three compartments fine furnishings have been removed and the elegant crimson colored silk with which the

entire insides were tufted and upholstered have been removed by the hands of vandals. Yet for all of this it is the old private coach of President Lincoln—the only railroad car ever built by the United States Government for the use of a President and cabinet. The visitors to the World's Fair who see it recognize in it a national treasure of incomparable value and rich association.

At the close of the war it was sold by the government to the Union Pacific Railroad Company, at Omaha, Neb. It has remained their property until the fall of 1903 when after seven years of negotiating it was sold for a large consideration to Mr. F. E. Snow who has placed it in the "Lincoln Museum" with most of the original furniture belonging to it, even to the old bed sofa which he slept on while on his tours and which (according to the late Geo. M. Pullman) was the forerunner of the berths in his now famous sleepers.

Extract from Clipping in

THE ST. LOUIS REPUBLIC: SUNDAY, MAY 1, 1904.

Of all the interesting exhibits at the World's Fair, there is none that has created more general attention or is viewed with a greater affection and reverence than the old "Lincoln Car" since its arrival and installation in the Lincoln Museum World's Fair grounds. None of the visitors at the museum who have had the privilege of seeing this sacred relic go away without gazing at the old coach for some time with evident affectionate interest, and very few look at it save with uncovered heads.

Although the car now is in a dilapidated condition, plainly showing that it has been abandoned to the cold storms of winter and the sun's hot rays of summer for too many years, it is still the car that was used to bear the remains of President Lincoln from Washington, D. C., to Springfield, Ill. for interment. Time has made sad changes within and without. From a beautifully decorated exterior, its sides are cracked and weather-beaten. Inside the several compartments fine furnishings have been removed and the elegant crimson colored silk with which the entire insides were tufted and upholstered has been removed by the hands of vandals. Yet for all this it is the old private car of President Lincoln—the only coach ever built by the United States Government for the use of a President and Cabinet. The visitors who see it recognize in it a national treasure of incomparable value and rich association.

The idea of building a private car for the use of President Lincoln and his Cabinet was first conceived in the War Department of the Government in the [illegible], and orders were [illegible] State Penitentiary

Built for the use of President Lincoln by the United States Government in the U.S. Military Car Shops, at Alexandria, Va., in 1863–1864.

Conveyed Mr. Lincoln's remains from Washington, D. C. to Springfield, Ills., for burial in 1865.

THE HISTORIC "LINCOLN CAR."

FRANKLYN B. SNOW,

LINCOLN MUSEUM,
WORLD'S FAIR 1904,
ST. LOUIS, MO.

Purchased from the Government by the Union Pacific Railroad Co. in 1866.

Purchased from the Union Pacific Railroad Co. by Franklyn B. Snow in 1903.

On exhibition in the Lincoln Museum, World's Fair 1904.

ST. LOUIS, March 20th, 1904.

Mr. H. E. Barker
   Springfield, Ill.

My Dear Sir,

   Yours of the 4th Inst. at hand. It is my expectation to be in Springfield before the opening of the Fair Mr. Barker and I will call on you and see what we can do. In the mean time I wish you would let me know if the picture you have of the engine and car is the "Lincoln Car" or the car that was known as the "Guards Car" the "Lincoln Car" has the U.S. coat of arms painted on the sides. I have four different photos of the car, two of which was taken by the Govt. photographer. If you will send me a Photo copy of the car and engine I will send you in return a photo (and a fine one) of the car about 8 x 12 in size, this one was taken by the Govt. and shows the car decorated in mourning ready for the journey to Springfield, it was taken at

THE HISTORIC "LINCOLN CAR."

FRANKLYN B. SNOW.

LINCOLN MUSEUM,
WORLD'S FAIR 1904,
ST. LOUIS, MO

Built for the use of President Lincoln by the United States Government in the U.S. Military Car Shops, at Alexandria, Va., in 1863-1864.
Conveyed Mr. Lincoln's remains from Washington, D. C. to Springfield, Ills., for Burial in 1865.

Purchased from the Government by the Union Pacific Railroad Co. in 1866.
Purchased from the Union Pacific Railroad Co. by Franklyn B. Snow in 1903.
On exhibition in the Lincoln Museum, World's Fair 1904.

2

ST. LOUIS, _____ 1904.

the U.S. Military Car Shops in Alexandria, Va. and shows the shops with Guards and Etc. ready for the journey. Have you anything that could be sold as relics with a profit? Is the list of articles you sent me in your last letter the articles you have on sale regularly? Kindly let me hear from you as soon as possible and oblige,

Yours truly,
F. B. Snow
3131 Lucas Ave.
St. Louis Mo.

THE HISTORIC "LINCOLN CAR"
NOW OWNED BY F. B. SNOW.

Built for the use of President Lincoln by the United States Government at the U. S Military Car Shops, at Alexandria, Va., in 1863-1864.

Conveyed Mr. Lincoln's remains from Washington, D C, to Springfield, Ill, for burial in 1865

Purchased from the Government by the Union Pacific Railroad Co in 1866.

Purchased from the Union Pacific Railroad Co by Franklin B Snow in 1905

On exhibition in the Lincoln Museum, World's Fair, 1904

From Government photograph taken at the United States Military Car Shops, Alexandria, Va, April 20th, 1865 After being draped to receive the body of Mr Lincoln and while awaiting orders to move to Washington, D C, six miles away to receive the remains The military guards can be seen on duty

LINCOLN'S PRIVATE CAR FOR CHICAGO PARK.

Oct 5 1905

President Lincoln's private car, which has been exhibited at most of the big expositions held in this country during recent years, is now standing upon a side track in the Chicago & Alton Ry. yards at Joliet, Ill. The custodian of the car has offered to give it to the Lincoln Park commission of Chicago.

FAMOUS COACH DESTROYED

Carriage Was Made Before Lincoln's Time. 1909

NEW CASTLE, Pa., Feb. 3.—The historic "Lincoln" coach in which President Lincoln is said to have ridden to Washington for his inauguration, was destroyed in a fire at Sharpsville, Pa. It was the sole passenger equipment of the little Sharpsville railroad, running between that town and Washington Junction. It was covered with sheetiron, put on before Lincoln made his famous ride and was supposed to be bullet proof.

A recent dispatch from Minneapolis tells of the burning of the Lincoln funeral car, the car which carried the body of the war president from Washington to Springfield. This car, which was used also as the private car of President Lincoln during the war, was purchased by Thomas Lowry six years ago and taken to a Minneapolis suburb. A few days ago a prairie fire swept over ten blocks of ground in this suburb, igniting the historic relic and burned it into a mass of charred wood and iron. 1911

no date or source

BURNING OF THE LINCOLN FUNERAL CAR.
Famous car which brought body of martyr President from Washington to Springfield, Ill., in April, 1865, recently destroyed by fire at Minneapolis, where it had been kept since 1895.

LINCOLN COACH BURNS

New Castle, Pa., Feb. 4.—The historic Lincoln coach in which President Lincoln rode to Washington for his inaugural was destroyed in a fire yesterday at Sharpsville, Pa.

SHOOK HANDS WITH LINCOLN.
St. Petersburg, Fla., Dec. 25—(*P*)—Colonel Maximilian Brueckman is 91 but the time he shook hands with Abraham Lincoln is fresh in his memory. It was in 1864, in Philadelphia. —1935—

Lincoln Car Burns
The Lincoln funeral car, the car which in April, 1865, carried the body of Abraham Lincoln from Washington to its final resting place in Springfield, Ill., is a mass of charred wood and iron. The car, which has been visited by hundreds of thousands of Americans, was destroyed by a prairie fire which swept through ten blocks in Columbia Heights. The car was purchased by Thomas Lowry in 1905, and brought to Minneapolis. It was used as the private car of Lincoln and his cabinet during the last three years of the civil war.

The articles are pasted on p. opposite the inside back cover of copy 5 of Oldroyd's Words of Lincoln. The book was originally owned by a lady living in St. Paul, MN.

Panels - Lincoln funeral car - Gettysburg Cir

Q. What became of the Lincoln funeral car? T. H. C.
A. The Lincoln funeral car was preserved for many years and then broken up by the Pullman company. One of the marked features of the car was a series of landscapes painted on wooden panels between the car windows. Mr. Pullman preserved some of the best of them, and presented them to his friends. So far as is known no other parts of the car remain.

No. 31   THE LINCOLN FUNERAL CAR.

America - 1862-65

When President Lincoln assumed office, the necessity for providing a special car for his personal use, at once became apparent, for travelling back & forth as his position required made it more convenient for meeting delegations, sleeping at night, his dining periods and for general all around comfort and for his convenience. Much valuable time could also be saved, for the car provided with its file cases, could convey necessary documents made available for use when they were needed.

A car was found on one of the railroads, which, when a few changes were made suited the President and Mrs. Lincoln, who at times accompanied the President on his journeys. The car was used more probably on the Baltimore and Ohio RR than on other railroad. When the assassination of the President occurred in April 1865, the question of providing a suitable car to convey the body from Washington to Springfield became imperative, but Mr. Myron Lamson foreman of the B&O Car Yards at Washington soon solved that problem, by securing permission to have a few minor changes made in the President's car, and these were made at once, making the car suitable for conveying the body on a catafalque in the center of the parlor end of the car, from which it could easily be removed, when special services held in Memory of the President were celebrated, and replaced on the catafalque in the car. And so it was used, and no special care being provided for it, it was recently (1930) destroyed by fire. Its peculiar construction can be seen at a glance.

Mr. Lamson the Yard foreman in Washington of the B&O RR was also a member of the Washington City Home guards and is seen in the photograph standing on the front end of the car. He was one of the guards of honor.

E. P. Baugh

BUILT FOR LINCOLN; BORE HIS REMAINS

PRESIDENT'S PRIVATE CAR WAS USED BUT ONCE.

Constructed as an Aid to His Business and Pleasures It Served Only to Bear His Murdered Body to His Grave—A Splendid Specimen of Its Day.

It was the irony of fate that the first private car for the use of a President of the United States should be used by him only as a vehicle to bear him to his grave. Such was the case with the car built for Abraham Lincoln.

Shortly before the assassination of Lincoln the company in charge of the construction of the car notified the President that the car was in readiness for his use and preparations were made for it to be transferred to the national Capital from the construction yards. It arrived in Washington just in time to be fitted up as the national funeral car. The car was the first ever constructed for a President and was the handsomest railway car in existence when it was finished. The fittings were sumptuous and with its observation platform and system of heating new to the cars of the period it marked a distinct advance in railway construction.

Arrived in Washington the remodelling of the car began under the direction of Myron H. Lamson. The lounge which had been constructed in the front end of the car was draped in black and here lay the body of the martyred hero on its journey, first to New York City and then across the country to its last resting place. The exterior of the car was heavily draped with black, looped with heavy cord and tassels. The exterior of the car bore a large American emblem on one side while the axles of the undertrucks were covered with large protectors in the shape of the American eagle. Large platforms were at each end of the car.

On April 21 after the most impressive obsequies, the car, bearing the President's remains, with six other cars and the locomotive all heavily draped in black slowly moved out of Washington amid a dense crowd of silent and heavy hearted spectators. Up to that date the history of this country had never before recorded so sad a spectacle as the passing of this funeral train across the country. Since two more such caravans of sorrow have held the eyes of the American people as they wended their way to the last resting places of the great dead.

In city and country the funeral train was greeted by vast and silent crowds while in the larger cities thousands passed through the car and took a last look at the face of the martyred President. On May 3, the train reached Springfield, Ill., and on the following day as a chorus sang "Peace, Troubled Soul" the casket was closed. The funeral car was returned to the yards of the Pennsylvania Railroad Company in Washington and was later reconstructed and used as a regular passenger coach.

LINCOLN'S FUNERAL CAR.

CONGER

San Diego Resident One of Builders of Famous Funeral Car

Photograph of railroad car built for the personal use of President Abraham Lincoln, and which became his funeral car. James T. Barkley, now a resident of San Diego, was one of the builders of this car.

On April 14, 1865, exactly four years after the surrender of Fort Sumter, when everything looked hopeful and the Civil war was over, President Abraham Lincoln was shot, and a day later died, and the nation was plunged into mourning.

The car illustrated above had recently been built for the president and his cabinet. It became his funeral car, and on April 21, after most impressive obsequies, this car, heavily draped and bearing the president's remains, moved out of Washington amid a vast throng of silent and sad spectators.

Myran H. Lamson, an enlisted mechanic and superintendent of the Orange and Alexandria railroad, served as director during the construction of this car, and James T. Barkley, now a resident of San Diego, also an enlisted officer, upon the recommendation of Gen. Thomas Holt, was detailed, together with Lawrence O'Day, a citizen of Binghamton, N. Y., to build the car. A room was partitioned off in the car shop, and no one allowed to enter except to bring in material. The car had double trucks, with broad tread wheels to enable it to run over nearly all railroads in the United States. The color, when finished, was a dark olive, with a large oval panel on either side, in which was painted the United States coat of arms. This car was finished and run out over the Orange and Alexandria railroad on a trial trip to Warenton Junction and pronounced a perfect success.

On the trial trip were President Lincoln, Secretary of State Seward, Gen. McCullum, who had charge of all military railroads in the United States; Myran H. Lamson, superintendent of railroads, and Lawrence O'Day and James T. Barkley, builders of the car.

RAILROAD CAR Built for Lincoln

BUILT CAR FOR LINCOLN.

California Says President Sat on Sawhorse to Watch Work.

SAN DIEGO, Cal., Feb. 12 (ʒ).— Memories of the Civil War, when he was assigned to build a private railroad car for President Lincoln, were recalled here today by James T. Barkley, a 90-year-old veteran.

"In December, 1863, I was detailed, on recommendation of General McCallum, by General Thomas Holt, to build a new car for the President," said Mr. Barkley.

Assisted by a civilian and an enlisted mechanic, Barkley said, he went to work in a room in the government shops at Alexandria, Va.

"Lincoln would visit us two or three times a month during construction," said Mr. Barkley. "Sitting on a sawhorse, he would suggest changes. There were many suggestions. In the rear of the car was a conference room. In the middle was Lincoln's quarters; in the front a wash room. The car was upholstered in red plush. The work was finished the third week in May."

Eleven months later, Mr. Barkley said, the car, heavily draped and bearing Lincoln's body in a sealed casket, moved out of Washington for Illinois.

BARKLEY, JAMES T.

N. Y. Times
2/13/30

How the Lincoln Funeral Car Was Built

By G. F. Starbuck, *Boston and Maine Railroad**

IN the February issue of the Baltimore and Ohio MAGAZINE there appeared a very interesting picture and description of the Lincoln Funeral Car in which the author says, "What became of the car afterward I do not know."

It was purchased by Vice President Durant of the Union Pacific Railroad.

The construction of the car was begun in November, 1863, at Alexandria, Va., and was completed in February, 1865. The inside length was forty-two feet, and it was divided into a drawing room, a state room (in the center) and a parlor, the drawing room and parlor being connected by an aisle at one side of the car. The sides and ends were upholstered from the seat rail to the head lining. The upper deck was painted white with the coat of arms of the various states in the panels.

The body bolsters were trussed, and the brass nuts on the ends of the truss rods clearly show in the picture. The trucks of each pair were connected by a truss carrying the main center plate at its center, the ends of the truss connected to guide center plates with curved slots, one on each truck. There were eight side bearings of spring steel and rubber. The wheels were of cast iron, thirty-three inches in diameter, and the truck wheel base was four feet ten inches.

The outside of the car was painted a rich chocolate brown; in the oval panel was the coat of arms of the United States, and above it in small gold letters, "United States." There was also some gold ornamentation.

The running gear was so different from the customary type that an attendant with tools and repair parts accompanied it on the funeral train. The car contained, in addition to the remains of President Lincoln, those of his son, which had been disinterred. When the car was returned to Alexandria the black crepe drapery was removed, boxed, and sent to the Treasury Department.

The great Pacific Railway excursion of 1866 celebrated the attainment of the 100th meridian, the 247th mile post, reached by the Union Pacific in 182 working days. Among the company were Vice President Durant, Rutherford B. Hayes, George Francis Train, George M. Pullman, Robert T. Lincoln, and many other noted railroad men, government officials, editors, photographers and distinguished guests. Next to the rear car was the Lincoln car, occupied by Mr. Durant and his personal party.

Mr. Durant later acquired a Pullman car, and the Lincoln car was placed occasionally thereafter at the disposal of government commissioners.

The latest picture which I have of the car shows it with two equalizer trucks. Truss rods had been added and new bolsters near the ends of the car; but the nuts on the ends of the original bolsters were still visible. The oval panels had been removed from the sides and plain handrails replaced the original ornamental ones.

*Mr. Starbuck is in the Mechanical Engineering Department of the Boston and Maine and has on several occasions contributed interesting information to our MAGAZINE. The Lincoln funeral car is still in the possession of the Union Pacific Railroad.

The Lincoln Funeral Car

By William H. Lamson

THE Lincoln funeral car was built in the first place for the use of President Lincoln, and was kept in the yards of the Baltimore and Ohio Railroad Company in Washington, D. C. My father, Myron H. Lamson, was an enlisted mechanic in the service of the road at that time, and served as assistant foreman during the construction of the car. After the assassination of Mr. Lincoln, he supervised the alterations which were made in the car that it might properly receive the casket and remains.

After the body had lain in state at the Capitol, it was taken to the Baltimore and Ohio station and placed on a catafalque in the center of the car. On April 21, 1865, the train, consisting of this and six other cars, headed by the engine and tender all heavily draped in black, pulled out of Washington. A great throng of reverent patriots witnessed the departure, the silence being broken only by the noise of the train and the sobs of the multitude. The train went north via Baltimore, and during the long trip passed through many of the great cities of the Union, where the people had assembled, and with reverent silence paid their tribute to the martyred President. The end of the journey was reached on May 3, 1865, at Springfield, Illinois. After lying in state under the dome of the Capitol of Illinois for several days, the burial took place in Springfield.

What became of the car afterwards, I do not know. My father is seen in the picture, standing on the platform in his uniform, while he was acting as one of the guard of honor. The day before, he had engaged a photographer to take a picture of the car as it lay in the yard, and after he had ordered a dozen pictures, he purchased the negative, which has been in my family ever since.

When the Grand Army of the Republic held its annual reunion in 1908, one of these original pictures was loaned to them, and a post card negative was made from which a great number of cards were printed with a small portrait of President Lincoln and a short description of the car printed up in one corner of the card on the face side, the picture of the car covering the entire back of the card.

This same picture was loaned to E. L. Bangs, of the Baltimore and Ohio Railroad, who made a 5 x 7 plate negative from it and returned the picture to me. The photographs obtained from this negative are good and compare very favorably with the pictures made from the original negative.

THE LINCOLN FUNERAL CAR

Built for the use of President Lincoln, this car, when in Washington, was kept in the yards of the Baltimore and Ohio. Its conversion into a funeral car was supervised by Myron H. Lamson, an enlisted (war-time) mechanic in our service. Mr. Lamson, who is standing on the platform in this photo, was the father of the author of the story

Gaskill Music Company
PIANOS — RADIOS
SHEET MUSIC — RECORDS
NEBRASKA CITY, NEBRASKA   Nov. 13, 1934

Lincoln Life Insurance Co
Fort Wayne Ind
Gentlemen:

Enclosed find a small piece of upholstering which please help identify if possible. I have another piece of the same material from another source the size ~ 3 X 1 inches.

The piece enclosed came from Sioux City Iowa and was in a small carved bone case with notation "This small piece of cloth from upholstering in the A. Lincoln funeral car"

The larger piece has been preserved for many years by a Nebraska City family and supposed to be from the chair in which President Lincoln was assassinated.

If you can help in any way to identify this, it will be greatly appreciated. I think surely this is an item that is connected in some way or would not have been preserved so long.

November 16, 1934

Mr. John E. Gaskill
Nebraska City, Nebraska

My dear Mr. Gaskill:

In reply to your inquiry about the piece of red tapestry which you enclosed in your letter and which we are returning, we find the following excerpt in the Union Pacific Magazine for February 1933:

> "When A. L. Mohler was President of the Union Pacific he found that this couch from the Lincoln car was stored at the Omaha shops. He had the old red upholstering removed and had it recovered in black leather and placed in his private office."

There is a picture of this old couch in this magazine and other information about the car which you might like to have.

I suggest that you write the Union Pacific Magazine, 130 Union Pacific Building, Omaha, Nebraska, and ask if a copy of the publication is available.

                Very truly yours,

LAW:LH   Director
Enc.

1935

CHICAGO HISTORICAL SOCIETY
Founded in 1856
Clark Street and North Avenue
LINCOLN PARK

OFFICERS
CHARLES B. PIKE .... President
HENRY J. PATTEN .... First Vice-President
FRANK I. LOESCH .... Second Vice-President
CECIL BARNES .... Secretary
PAUL S. RUSSELL .... Treasurer
L. H. SHATTUCK .... Director

EARLY AMERICAN BUILDINGS

The Milton S. Osborne sketches of early buildings in the United States, now on display in the Current Exhibit Room, are causing a great deal of comment. Professor Osborne, who holds the chair of architecture at the University of Manitoba, has lent the Society fifty-two of his beautiful sketches portraying the history of American architecture from 1700 to 1845.

Buildings from eight different states are shown in the collection. Illinois is well represented with nine sketches, among which are the First State Capitol at Vandalia, the First Presbyterian Church at Galena, the Court House of Mt. Vernon, and the First National Bank of Shawneetown. Thomas Jefferson's beloved "Monticello," President Monroe's home, "Ashlawn," and the State Capitol at Richmond have a place with the Virginia sketches. Among the historic houses of Alabama are the Samuel Mintern Peck Home and the Gorgas House. Tennessee's contribution is "The Hermitage," the home of Andrew Jackson at Nashville. All of the South Carolina drawings, sixteen in number, show the city of Charleston, and include the Rutledge Plantation, the Colonel John Stuart House, the Old Exchange Building, and the Miles Brewton House. The Old Exchange Building and the Miles Brewton House, which are still standing today, have been converted into museums open to the public. The Library Court-yard at Salem College, with its red brick walls and green shutters is characteristic of North Carolina.

We have in this exhibit a panorama of early American architecture demonstrating vividly English, French, Dutch, and Roman influence. The sketches are delicately colored in soft crayon, although a few of them are done in black and gray. Here details of low southern mansions, towering church steeples, massive pillars, beautiful arches and winding stairways, all tell of their role in American architecture.

MURALS FOR LEE HALL

The Art Department of the Society under the direction of Staff Artist Hans Werner is developing a series of murals for the Lee Stair Hall. In working out the series of twelve paintings, it was decided to choose the most interesting and outstanding events in American history. The first of the murals, which approximate 10 ft. x 9 ft. in size, depicts the landing of the Pilgrim Fathers on the bleak and barren New England coast with the *Mayflower* in the distance. The emotions of the landing party are vividly portrayed. The second mural represents a critical moment during the discussions of the Declaration of Independence and shows John Adams, Thomas Jefferson, Benjamin Franklin, and Charles Thomson talking with John Hancock, President of the Continental Congress. Seated in the background are many other famous members of that body. The figures are almost life-size, and a special effort at accuracy has been made in the matter of the faces.

NEW MEMBERS

The following persons were elected to membership in the period from December 1, 1934 to April 10, 1935:

Honorary Life Members — Mrs. Bernhard Rosenberg, Austin Selz, Frank E. Selz, Mrs. J. Harry Selz, Addison Stillwell.

Governing Life Member—Albert Blake Dick, Jr.

Life Members—Graham Aldis, Mrs. Gertrude Briggs, Mrs. C. Frederick Childs, Mrs. Hugo Dalmar, Mrs. C. Morse Ely, Judge Ross C. Hall, Dr. Clarence Hennan, Mrs. Leonard D. Karcher, Mrs. George T. Langhorne, Douglas C. McMurtrie, Mrs. Langdon Pearse, Daniel Peterkin, Mr. and Mrs. Paul S. Russell, Jean Shedd Schweppe, John Shedd Schweppe.

Annual Members—Eugene A. Bournique, W. R. Bowes, Robert O. Calvert, Ernest E. East, Mrs. Frank M. Elliott, Rev. Eneas B. Goodwin, Mrs. Robert H. Hunter, Mrs. Walter H. Huth, John E. Jensen, J. Farren MacMahon, Dr. Benjamin H. Orndoff, Guy S. Osborn, Mrs. Marguerite H. Robertson, Mrs. Donald M. Ryerson, Mrs. Harry H. Shearson, James G. Skinner, W. Edwin Stanley, W. J. Stelzer, Mrs. Leroy T. Vernon, Joseph F. Wanberg, Miss Katherine Wolcott, George Zaphirio.

MUSEUM GIFTS

Three branched crystal candelabra. On exhibit in British Colonial Room.

Three dozen teaspoons, three dozen cups and saucers, and three dozen small plates—pattern Colonial Times by Crown Ducat, England. To be used for teas and receptions. Gift of Mrs. Charles B. Pike.

Table lamp and marble-top table from the Orrington Lunt house. On exhibit in the Victorian Room. Given in the name of Miss Cornelia Gray Lunt.

Early 18th century loom from an old house in Hartford, Connecticut, of that period. Gift of Mrs. H. D. Harris.

Portrait of Mrs. Arthur Burr Meeker (Mary Louise Griggs) by Cogswell. Gift of Mrs. Arthur Meeker and Mrs. Davis S. Cook, Jr.

LIBRARY GIFTS

Journals and sermons of Jeremiah Porter. Gift of Mr. Sherman M. Goble.

Letters of General U. S. Grant chiefly to his daughter Nellie. Gift of the Estate of Frank Hatch Jones.

Broadside announcing campaign speech of Abraham Lincoln, April 9, 1840. Gift of Mr. Douglas C. McMurtrie.

Narrative of the Adventures of Senas Leonard, written by himself. Gift of Mr Joseph Adams.

Miscellaneous manuscripts including John Whistler document, Steuben items, etc. Gift of Dr. Otto L. Schmidt.

Collection of Lincolniana including 78 volumes in fine bindings. Gift of Mrs. James Ward Thorne.

Souvenir of Chicago Day—Monday, October 9, 1899. Gift of Mr. Cyrus H. McCormick.

The Life of George Washington — Maps and Subscribers Names. Philadelphia, C. P Wayne, 1807. Gift of Mr. Charles B. Pike.

LINCOLN FUNERAL CAR
Judge James N. Wilkerson

In November, 1863, the Government Military Car Shops at Alexandria, Virginia, began construction of a specially designed private car for the use of the President of the United States. The exigencies of wartime retarded progress so greatly, however, that it was not until the spring of 1865 that it was finished.

On April 14, 1865, according to Mr. W. H H. Price, Shop Superintendent, General J. H Devereux and Mr. Jameson were anxiously awaiting President Lincoln's reply to their invitation to come to Alexandria to inspect the car and give it his approval before it left the shops. Their pride in their work was rudely shattered, however, by the news of Lincoln's assassination. Sadly the workmen sent the car on to Washington to be used in the funeral train.

To insure greater safety the car had been equipped with four trucks instead of the regulation two, and proved so difficult to operate that only by exercising the greatest care would it pass switch points. On the trip to Springfield, Illinois, a mechanic with duplicate parts and special tools had to accompany the car to keep it running on schedule. After the Springfield funeral, it was returned to Chicago where the surplus trucks were removed. This done, it was forwarded to Washington where it was locked and placed in storage with all furnishings and equipment intact. In 1866 it was auctioned off with some surplus war material and was purchased by the Union Pacific Railroad through the efforts of Mr. Sidney Dillon, a director. The furnishings of the car are now on exhibit at the General Offices of the Union Pacific in Omaha.

About 1870 the Colorado Central Railroad bought the funeral car and used it in their passenger service for several years. Later it was retired and used as an office car for construction crews. While standing unguarded on a sidetrack in western Kansas one day, vandals stripped it of everything removable. In 1879 the Colorado Central was absorbed by the Union Pacific System. The car was shown at the Trans-Mississippi Exposition in Omaha and attracted wide attention.

About 1900 a showman, one Franklin B. Snow, managed in some way to buy it. The car made him a fortune when he exhibited it at the St. Louis World's Fair. In 1905 Hon. Thomas Lowery bought it and presented it to the City of Minneapolis with impressive ceremonies. Here for six years it was displayed to the public on a lot provided by the municipality. A careless smoker dropped a burning cigarette into the dry grass of the lot on March 18, 1911, and the fire spread uncontrolled to the shed. The car was quickly destroyed. By coincidence it was almost forty-six years to the day from the afternoon on which it had stood so bravely shining awaiting inspection by President Lincoln.

LAKE PORTS IN 1850
(Continued from Page 1)

us—when we start for the West on Tuesday we shall probably enter some of the best lands in the state. . . We have a kind of fish called the White fish served on our table here, which I think the nicest I ever tasted. The mutton is not good as far as I have had of it—beef and hams are good—butter about middling—they dont put in the right kind of salt. . . my clothes are very much soiled with dust—it is so dry here—crops are suffering. There is a fresh breeze here from the lakes almost constantly during the year —it is bad for those with weak lungs. . .

Your affectionate father, J. Bowen

Two Rare Lincoln Pictures

Ill. St. Journal 6-30-36

These two rare Lincoln pictures have been enlarged from tintypes. The funeral car (above) was built for the Civil war president four months before his assassination. He had taken only a few trips in it before he was shot. At his death, the car was taken across the Potomac to the plant in which it was built and draped for the journey to Springfield.

Upon its arrival in Springfield with the remains of Mr. Lincoln it was switched to the Chicago and Alton yards where it remained for some time. Afterward it was purchased by officials of the Union Pacific railroad and used by them until it was considered too old. It was then transferred to the Colorado service of the road and for a time was in the yards at Omaha. With the opening of the first world's fair at Chicago it was taken to that city and shown with other Lincoln relics near the Illinois building.

Fire consumed the historic coach some time after the close of the exposition.

The picture of the mourning-draped Lincoln home was taken by a person in a delegation of 100 persons who came to Springfield to attend the funeral services for Mr. Lincoln.

Funeral Car

DAILY MAGAZINE
Oakland Tribune
MONDAY, FEBRUARY 12, 1940

STRANGE AS IT SEEMS — By John Hix

"CANDIDE" — VOLTAIRE'S MOST POPULAR ROMANCE, WAS WRITTEN IN 3 DAYS!

GOLDFISHES HAVE THEIR TEETH IN THEIR THROATS

CHARLES HALL — DROVE A GOLF BALL INTO A CADDY'S MOUTH! — Scioto Club, Columbus, Ohio, 1926 —

ABRAHAM LINCOLN — MADE ONLY ONE TRIP IN A LUXURIOUS PRIVATE RAILWAY CAR BUILT FOR HIS PERSONAL USE — AND THAT WAS AFTER HIS DEATH! HE STEADFASTLY REFUSED TO ACCEPT OR RIDE IN THE CAR DURING HIS LIFETIME...

LINCOLN'S DEATH CAR
Strange as it seems, the luxuriously appointed funeral car that conveyed assassinated President Lincoln's body from Washington to Springfield, Ill., was built by the United States Military Railroad at Alexandria, Va., to carry him to and from Civil War front lines. The car contained every available convenience. An important addition to Lincoln's funeral cortege was George M. Pullman's famous Pioneer. Wider than the standard car of the time, the Pioneer's use necessitated the immediate widening of clearance past station platforms and bridges.

Bulletin of The Lincoln National Life Foundation . . . Dr. R. Gerald McMurtry, Editor
Published each month by The Lincoln National Life Insurance Company, Fort Wayne, Indiana

Number 1431   FORT WAYNE, INDIANA   May, 1957

THE LINCOLN FUNERAL CAR

The railway car, which carried President Lincoln's remains from Washington, D. C., to Springfield, Illinois, in the spring of 1865, was considered a triumph of the car builder's art. On the one thousand six hundred and sixty-two mile funeral route, over a million people saw and admired this beautiful railway coach. However, it had not been designed originally as a funeral car, but as a private presidential car for the Chief Executive.

The idea of building a private car for the use of President Lincoln and his cabinet was first conceived by the War Department, and it was built under the supervision of Colonel D. C. McCallum, Superintendent of Military Railroads, at the United States Military Car Shops at Alexandria, Virginia. Because President Lincoln did considerable traveling, it was thought that a special railway car for his own personal use would be fitting for his position, as well as efficient for the conduct of the affairs of his office.

The car as originally constructed was forty-two feet long and eight and one-half feet wide. It had a raised roof like modern coaches with circular ends. It was divided into three compartments. A door in the vestibule of the coach opened into a narrow passageway which extended the entire length of the car along one side. From this passageway, doors opened into each of the three private rooms.

A room in the rear end of the car, the stateroom, was considerably larger than the others, and it was furnished with a large sofa and reclining chairs. The small rooms were also provided with sofas and chairs, although somewhat inferior to those in the larger room.

The large compartment was to be used as the President's office and study, where he could entertain guests and transact business with officials of the government and officers of the armed services.

The seven and one-half foot sofa was a combination affair and was made of unusual length to accommodate the elongated form of the President. Used as a sofa or lounge during the day, it could be adjusted at night into a double bed of two berths, upper and lower, like berths in a sleeping car. This especially constructed sofa, according to George M. Pullman, was the forerunner of the berths used in Pullman sleeping cars today.

The walls of each of the compartments were padded with rich, corded crimson silk upholstery, reaching halfway to the ceiling. The upper deck, between the transoms, contained panels on which were painted coats of arms of the several states then forming the Union. The woodwork above the doors and windows on the interior was painted zinc white with decorations in gold and the national colors. Below the windows, the woodwork was of natural wood, oak and walnut. The curtains were of light-green silk.

On the outside, occupying a space five feet by two feet, were two oval shaped panels or medallions, of metal, on which was painted the coat of arms of the United States. Above the oval panels, between the windows, in small gold letters were the words "United States." The car's exterior was likely first painted a rich maroon color highlighted with decorations of gold leaf. However, when it was reconditioned as Lincoln's funeral coach, it was probably painted a dark olive color. The axles of the under trucks were covered with large protectors resembling, rather grotesquely, the shape of the American eagle.

The car was said to be ironclad, the armor plate being set in between the inner and outer walls, rendering it bullet-proof. This precaution, however, appears to have been of little consequence unless the window glass was also bullet-proof. Some of the men assisting in the construction of the coach in their reminiscences stated that "no armor was used in its construction." Nevertheless, the car was of such great weight that its builders thought it necessary to mount it on four, four-wheeled trucks. Because of its extreme weight and the manner in which it was mounted, "it rode . . . poorly."

The trucks were equipped with broad tread wheels to enable the car to run over nearly all gauge railroads in the United States. The large observation platform and the system of heating was new to the cars of that period and it marked a distinct advance in railway construction.

THE FUNERAL CAR
Photo taken at Chicago on the Lake Front, near Park Row, May 1, 1865, while on the way to Springfield with Mr. Lincoln's remains.

James T. Barkley of San Diego, California, in his reminiscences published in the *New York Times*, December 13, 1930, wrote: "In December, 1863, I was detailed on recommendation of General McCallum, by General Thomas Holt, to build a new car for the president." Barkley stated that the rear of the car was to be Lincoln's quarters and the front room a washroom.

Some of the men assigned to the construction of the car were W. H. Price, the foreman of the car shops, Lawrence O'Day, Nate Irwin, Myron H. Lamson, and Dennis O'Day. James T. Barkley and James Allen were the carpenters and Sergeant Robert Pierce was the artist and painter. Robert Cunningham worked on the trucks. According to Barkley, the car was completed the third week in May, 1864.

After making one trial trip over the Orange and Alexandria Railroad to Warrenton Junction, the car stood unused in the shops where it was constructed, although it was pronounced a perfect success.

It was erroneously reported years later that President Lincoln, Secretary of State Seward, Gen. McCallum, Myron H. Lamson, Lawrence O'Day and James T. Barkley made the trial run to Warrenton Junction.

Evidently Lincoln preferred not to travel in an armored car of luxurious appointments. Certain newspapers of New York took up the matter of the "presidential car" and were ready to chide Lincoln for such pretentiousness. How much this newspaper publicity influenced him, it is impossible to say, but he steadfastly refused to accept the car or to ride in it during his lifetime, even though he was notified that the car was in readiness for his use and preparations were underway to have it transferred to the nation's capital.

With the assassination and death of Lincoln, and the family's decision that the remains were to be taken to Springfield, Illinois, orders were issued by the War Department on April 18, 1865 to the officers in charge of the Military Car Shops in Alexandria, Virginia, to provide a suitable funeral car.

Myron H. Lamson, a member of the Washington City Home Guards and an enlisted mechanic in the service of the Baltimore and Ohio Railway Company, had a solution to the problem of the selection of a suitable funeral car. Having served as assistant foreman during the construction of the "presidential coach" and being familiar with the details of the car's interior, Lamson secured permission to make a few minor alterations which would make the car suitable for this imperative need. As Lamson was employed in the Baltimore and Ohio car yards in Washington, he was in a position to assume authority.

Using the center of the stateroom which was now heavily draped in black with heavy cords and tassels for the location of a hastily constructed catafalque, it was deemed possible to remove the remains with little difficulty, when special memorial services were held in the different cities along the route. At the same time, it would be easy to securely mount the coffin on the stationary catafalque while the train was in motion. The catafalque was shaped like a pyramid with a railing surrounding it, and it was possible for people to view the remains in the car. At the foot of Lincoln's casket was placed a smaller coffin, that of Willie Lincoln, the son who died in the White House in 1862. At Mrs. Lincoln's request, the dead father and son were to be interred in a vault in Springfield. Mrs. Lincoln was too ill to make the funeral journey.

With the necessary interior construction completed, and with the exterior suitably draped with broadcloth and silver fringe, the car was moved across the Potomac River in the early morning of April 21, to the railway station in Washington and attached to the rear of the funeral train already in waiting. Later, the funeral car was placed as the second coach from the rear, the family and officials using the rear coach.

The same day, the train consisting of the funeral coach, baggage car and about four or five other passenger cars, headed by an engine and tender, all heavily draped in black, pulled out of Washington. The train traveled by way of Baltimore, Harrisburg, Philadelphia, Jersey City, New York, Albany, Buffalo, Cleveland, Columbus, Indianapolis and Chicago, arriving on May 3, at Springfield. At Springfield the car was switched to the Chicago and Alton yards where it remained for some time. Later on, the car was returned to the Military Car Shops in Alexandria.

In June of the same year the car was used to convey to Albany, New York, the remains of Mrs. William H. Seward, the wife of the Secretary of State, who died on the 21st of the month, in the capital city.

With the close of the Civil War the government put a great amount of its railroad material in the hands of an auction firm in Cincinnati, Ohio, and a part of the rolling stock was the Lincoln funeral car. Sidney Dillon, who was then president of the Union Pacific, was directly responsible for its purchase, although the actual purchase was made after spirited bidding by T. C. Durant, first vice-president of the U. P. Possibly Dillon appreciated the historical significance of the car, but one of the reasons they wanted this armored coach was to convert it into a pay car to avert the danger of outlaw attacks. Oddly enough, many bullet holes were found in the woodwork of the coach, years later.

Once in Omaha, Nebraska, the funeral car was a great curiosity, not only because it was Lincoln's funeral

(Continued on page 4)

THE FUNERAL CAR
This Union Pacific Railroad photograph of the dilapidated funeral car was made after its conversion into a passenger coach with two, four-wheeled trucks, instead of four.

"THE INFELICITIES OF LOOKING LIKE BOOTH"

While Lincoln's assassin was still at large, the *New York Tribune* of April 20, 1865 carried on its front page a startling story entitled "Booth In Pennsylvania." This wild rumor prompted Governor A. G. Curtin to issue a proclamation offering a reward of $10,000 for the arrest of John Wilkes Booth, if captured in the Keystone State.

The account of Booth in Pennsylvania was featured by *The World*, New York, N. Y.; in its April 21, 1865 issue. The story originated at Reading, Pennsylvania, on April 19, when it was believed that Booth was a passenger on a train that left that city at 6:00 p.m. for Pottsville.

A Reading citizen said that he first saw the suspected person in a saloon on Tuesday night in company with another, drinking freely. He followed the man until he got upon the moving train. At this point, the Reading man boarded the departing train and shook hands with the suspect and asked him "whether he was going up in the train." Upon his answering that "he was not" he explained that he would be back in Reading in a day or so. The stranger, during the course of the conversation colored-up several times, and appeared annoyed and desirous of avoiding observation.

The citizen, whose name was not revealed, said he was positive that this man was Booth, because he had known the actor for several years. Just as the train left the station the loyal citizen jumped off the passenger coach and notified several officials of the railroad. His failure to give the alarm at once was an annoying development with which the officials had to cope in effecting the capture.

Corroborating the amateur sleuth, Mr. Lyon, a United States detective, said that Booth actually came to Reading by train. Furthermore, the detective stated that Booth had been in Reading all day. Mr. Lyon, assisted by Mr. Miller, another detective, proceeded to trace the assassin. They followed him to the depot and ascertained that a man answering Booth's description got on the train which had left for Pottsville.

These developments were immediately made known to Mr. G. A. Nicholls, Superintendent of the Philadelphia and Reading Railroad. The first move to apprehend the fugitive was to telegraph to Port Clinton. Unfortunately, the telegraph operator was not at his post, so an engine was fired up, and the two detectives and the man who claimed to have seen Booth proceeded at full steam to overtake the regular train.

The locomotive did not overtake the regular train, but at Port Clinton they were informed that the man they described had gotten off the train at that station. But which way the fugitive went, no one appeared to know.

Telegrams were sent to all points along the line of the road, because the detectives did not know whether or not this elusive man took the Catawissa train. A dispatch was also sent to Tamaqua, to the conductor of the train. Meanwhile, Port Clinton was searched with "a fine tooth comb."

Detective Lyon next received a telegram from Conductor Bright, at Catawissa saying: "No such man came through on my train." However, upon the arrival of another train at Tamaqua, the conductor telegraphed: "The man is on the train." Another telegram was hastily sent to the next station for further information and with orders for the man's detention. The chase had now narrowed down in one direction and Mr. Lyon was fully satisfied that the elusive fugitive was Lincoln's assassin.

Lyon issued a description of the man as follows: "About five feet eight inches in height; black hair, cut short and inclined to curl; short black mustache; had cotton in both ears; wore a white felt hat; had a piece of crape on the left arm; wore a Lincoln badge on the right breast in mourning; and had on a black coat with common blue military pants."

G. A. Nicholls, the Railroad Superintendent, reported to S. Bradford, Esq., regarding his part in the investigation in a letter written at Reading on April 20:

"On my return from Pottsville, the representations to me last evening were such that I sent a special engine to Pottsville, after the up-evening passenger train; but the man had left the train at Auburn before the telegram could reach it. He then walked back to Port Clinton after dark, and stole his passage to Tamaqua on one of our coal trains last night. He is now caught at Tamaqua, where we telegraphed to look out for him, and will be held until identified. There has been some ground for suspicion that it is Booth."

With the suspect in custody, the man who said he knew Booth and had seen him in Reading, was taken before a justice of the peace to make an affidavit of his knowledge. At this point, the cloak-and-dagger affair became a farce. The citizen of Reading swore that he had only seen Booth once, and that was seven years ago in a theatre in Baltimore. What was more surprising, he did not now believe that the person apprehended at Tamaqua was Booth. Yet, heretofore, he stated positively that the man was Booth and that he knew him intimately. Needless to say, the alleged assassin whose name was not revealed, was released.

The account of this incident is of no historical importance, except to indicate the apprehension of the American people while Booth was a fugitive. In every community, any strange man resembling the handsome actor, was immediately under suspicion, until he could prove his innocence. Scores of innocent people were arrested and held temporarily until proper identification could be made.

One reputable Massachusetts citizen was mistaken so often for Booth, that he remained at home until the assassin was captured. The assassin was also "recognized" in Greensburg and Franklin, and in two other Pennsylvania towns. Then he was "seen" in Brooklyn, New York, two places in Maryland, and in Ohio, Illinois and Maine.

Perhaps, Pennsylvanians were just a little more concerned than most people about the escape route of the assassin, due to his knowledge of the oil regions of that state where he had suffered some severe losses in speculation.

ISSUE OF 1909 2-CENT STAMP

367

On January 22, 1909, Congress adopted a joint resolution reading: "Resolved by the Senate and House of Representatives of the United States of America in Congress assembled, That the Postmaster General is hereby authorized to design and issue a special postage stamp, of the denomination of 2-cents, in commemoration of the one-hundredth anniversary of the birth of Abraham Lincoln."

The stamp was designed in time to place it on sale on Lincoln's birthday, February 12.

A description of the stamp follows: "Size and Shape, the same as of the regular issue of postage stamps; color, red. The subject is a profile, within an ellipse on end, of the head of Lincoln from St. Gaudens' statue. A spray of laurel leaves appears on either side of the ellipse. Above the subject appears the words 'U. S. Postage.' Below, the ellipse is broken by a ribbon containing the dates of Lincoln's birth and the one-hundredth anniversary thereof (1809-Feb. 12-1909), with the denomination in words (Two-cents) beneath."

The two-cent Lincoln of 1909 can be classified as follows:

A 83	367	2¢ Carmine	Perf. 12
A 83	368	2¢ Carmine	Imperf.
A 83	369	2¢ Carmine	Bluish paper Perf. 12

This stamp was issued in coils for use in vending and affixing machines. These private perforations are by the U. S. Automatic Vending Co., Schermack, Mail-O-Meter and Brinkerhoff.

THE FUNERAL CAR (Continued from page 2) coach, but because it was considered the finest railway car ever constructed. Many thousands of people visited the car shops to see it. After the car ceased to be a curiosity, it apparently received, during the next three decades, very rough treatment.

In 1892 a company of men from New York sent an agent to Omaha with a proposal to purchase the car so as to exhibit it at the World's Fair. Satisfactory terms could not be agreed upon and the project was abandoned. The agent, in the beginning of the negotiations, desired to have proof of the authenticity of the car and while no sale was effected, Mr. I. H. Congdon, for many years master mechanic of the Union Pacific Railroad, in a lengthy letter to E. L. Lomax, general passenger agent of the road, recorded a detailed history of the car:

"The famous car was brought to Omaha in 1866, and was purchased for the Union Pacific by T. C. Durant. Sidney Dillon manifested great interest in the car in the early days of the road. I was in charge of the locomotive department of the Great Western Railroad of Illinois, at Springfield, during the war, and was there at the time president Lincoln's remains were brought there. The car had been used as the funeral car, and stood in the railroad yards during the time that Lincoln's body lay in state in the capitol building, and we had an opportunity of examining it closely. I remember identifying it as the same car when it came here in 1866. When first brought to Omaha it was used as a private car by the directors, but on account of its extreme weight and the manner in which it was mounted, it rode so poorly that they soon abandoned it. I have been over the road with Mr. Dillon in the Lincoln car, and heard him speak of it as being the one that the president used during the war, and in which his remains were brought to Springfield. Mr. S. H. Clark, now president of the Union Pacific, stated to me a good many years ago that Mr. Dillon desired some of the furniture of the car taken out and sent to New York and I saw that this request was carried out.

"The car was built as nearly as possible to suit Mr. Lincoln's idea and was so peculiar in construction as to give it individual characteristics."

A great many of the original furnishings of the car are today preserved in the Union Pacific Historical Museum, including the silver service, walnut bookcase, desk, and couch. One early account of the funeral car states that George M. Pullman secured some of the landscape paintings on wooden panels which were between the car windows. Pullman is said to have kept some of the best of the panels and presented others to his friends.

When the Union Pacific officials used the funeral car as their private coach, a special building was constructed at Omaha to house it while not in service. Finally, it was sidetracked and used by the Union Pacific division superintendents to live in, and in 1870, it was sold to the Colorado Central Railroad Company at the time of the construction of that road to Golden, Colorado. The funeral coach was then converted into an ordinary day coach for passenger service between Denver and Golden. Its reconditioning for passenger service likely consisted of stripping out its fine interior and mounting it on two, instead of four, four-wheeled trucks. In 1878, the Colorado Central Railroad was absorbed by the Union Pacific and the car came back under the management of that road.

Eventually, this "palace on wheels" was sent out on the mountain division of the Union Pacific, and was used as a dining-car for a construction gang.

An observer in 1893 saw the funeral car on a sidetrack under the Eleventh Street viaduct in Omaha. It had just arrived from North Platte where it had been for years. Painted along the top of the car were the words, "Colorado Central Railroad," while beneath the window there was painted, "work train." It was so worn with age and abuse in 1893 as to be almost beyond recognition as once the world's finest "parlor car."

The purpose in bringing the car to Omaha was to give it a thorough overhauling and to put it in the same condition as it was in 1865. Then it was to be taken to Chicago for exhibition at the World's Fair. Needless to state, the reconditioning of the car was not extensive.

The car was exhibited at Chicago in 1893, at the Trans-Mississippi Exhibition at Omaha in 1898, and at the St. Louis World's Fair in 1904. In 1898 the Railway Company placed the car on exhibition in the Transportation Building at the Omaha Exhibition. It was said to have been seen by 1,250,000 people and the famous relic was damaged considerably at this time by vandals. However, for many months it stood on the tracks near the railroad shops as cast-off rolling stock.

In 1900, the negroes of Omaha proposed to have the city council appropriate money to secure the car and have it restored as nearly as possible to its original condition. Further plans were to have it housed permanently in a special building. This movement was headed by Dr. M. O. Ricketts, a negro physician. Mayor Moores, a Civil War veteran, looked upon the idea with favor, but these plans did not materialize.

In 1903, the funeral car was purchased from the Union Pacific Railroad Company by Franklin B. Snow. Snow exhibited the car in the Lincoln Museum at the St. Louis World's Fair in 1904. The $15,000 museum building was erected just north of the Illinois State Building and near the great ferris wheel.

The *St. Louis Republic*, of May 1, 1904, made the following comments about the historic car: "Of all the interesting exhibits at the World's Fair, there is none that has created more general attention or is viewed with a greater affection and reverence than the old 'Lincoln Car' since its arrival and installation in the Lincoln museum, World's Fair grounds. None of the visitors at the museum who have had the privilege of seeing this sacred relic go away without gazing at the old coach for some time with evident affectionate interest, and very few look at it save with uncovered heads.

"Although the car now is in a dilapidated condition, plainly showing that it has been abandoned to the cold storms of winter and the sun's hot rays of summer for too many years, it is still the car that was used to bear the remains of President Lincoln from Washington, D. C. to Springfield, Ill. for interment. Time has made sad changes within and without. From a beautifully decorated exterior, its sides are cracked and weatherbeaten. Inside the several compartments, fine furnishings have been removed and the elegant crimson colored silk with which the entire insides were tufted and upholstered has been removed by the hands of vandals. Yet for all of this it is the old private car of President Lincoln—the only coach ever built by the United States Government for the use of a president and cabinet. The visitors who see it recognize in it a national treasure of incomparable value and rich association."

On October 5, 1905, an unidentified newspaper carried a story to the effect that Lincoln's private car was standing on a sidetrack in the Chicago and Alton Railway Yards at Joliet, Illinois. The statement was also made that the custodian of the car had offered to give it to the Lincoln Park Commission of Chicago. However, Snow exhibited the car in various cities after the World's Fair was closed. In an advertising folder he suggested that "upon the moment of the arrival of this sacred relic in the city fourteen salutes from cannon will boom forth a welcome—one for each letter forming the name ABRAHAM LINCOLN, and one following each hour throughout the entire day."

In the fall of 1905, Snow sold the car to the Hon. Thomas Lowry, who presented it to the city of Minneapolis, Minnesota. The car arrived in Minneapolis in late October, 1905 and was placed on exhibition in a railroad yard. On March 18, 1911, the grass in this area caught fire and the car was reduced to a twisted mass of iron and charred wood.

A model of the Lincoln car is now on display at the Union Pacific Historical Museum. It was constructed by the employees at the Omaha shops. Aside from pictures and photographs of the historic car, the model at the Museum is the only tangible record left of a fabulous project in railway history.

Union Pacific Welcomes:

Union Pacific Railroad extends to you a cordial welcome to our headquarters building and our historical museum. Here you will see many relics of early days of the west. Old six guns used by early day desperadoes—rifles used by pioneer railroaders defending themselves from marauding Indians—the tea set from Abraham Lincoln's private car and a host of other historical objects.

All these have been donated by employees or friends of Union Pacific and because of the interest shown, we have set this area to grace in the most graphic manner possible the rugged, adventuresome spirit of our western pioneers.

No. 924 is Gone...

LOCATED only a few steps off the lobby on the first floor of Union Pacific Railroad's 12-story headquarters building in downtown Omaha, Neb., the Union Pacific Museum is within easy reach of all visitors to the city.

U. P.'s unique museum got its start quite modestly in 1921 when Paul Rigdon, chief clerk in President Carl R. Gray's office, showed Mr. Gray part of the silver service from Lincoln's car, which had been gathering dust in a vault.

Mr. Gray decided to start a museum in a small office adjoining his quarters. For the next few years the collection grew rapidly until the office was overcrowded. The museum was moved to its present location on the main floor in 1939.

During that year the motion picture "Union Pacific" was premiered in Omaha with the celebration of Golden Spike Days. Mr. W. M. Jeffers was president of the railroad at the time and his interest in the museum and the celebration heightened interest in the historical exhibits.

Thousands of railroaders added items to the collection and with this huge army of historic collectors the displays grew rapidly.

One of the remarkable facts about the museum is that every item it contains was donated. But whether it's an original historic document signed by President Lincoln or an old link and pin coupler found buried in a switching yard, the Union Pacific Museum is unusual and significant in that it gives visitors a flavorful taste of the old West and the human history of the growth of a railroad which is acknowledged by historians as one of the most important events which led to the western way of life we enjoy today.

Proof of its popularity is the fact that well over half a million persons have inspected the displays. On hand always to greet visitors and answer their questions are Museum Director Mrs. Irene A. Keeffe and her assistant, Miss Erma M. Smatlan.

The free museum is open for visits from 9 a.m. to 5 p.m. Monday through Friday.

...But Not Forgotten!

Original U. P. Offices   Present Headquarters

TRACE THE HISTORY...

An extensive display of documents, maps and pictures—handily encased in glass swinging panels—provide visitors with easy access to the documentary history of the building of Union Pacific lines through the untamed west.

Mounted for easy viewing, the files include early maps of the territory (some hand drawn and beautifully illustrated), photographs that portray adventure in the West's development, an album of old locomotive photos, panels of early and foreign paper money and coins, the original telegram reporting the completion of rail construction through to Promontory, Utah, old newspapers marking special events in the history of the country, and a separate file on famous outlaws that made the early railroad life a hazardous one.

RAILROAD SECTION...

For devoted railroad fans the museum boasts several miniature locomotives and an unusual collection of locomotive pictures taken when steam engines were the undisputed champions of railroad power.

And there is a railroad library which was started in one huge bookcase and has now grown to fill an entire vault.

Swinging panels for historical documents, photos

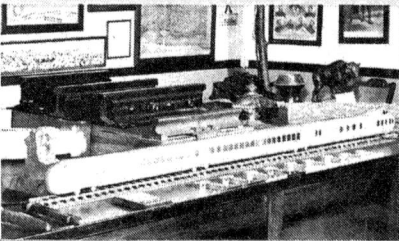
U. P.'s 1934 Streamliner—America's First

PIONEERS REPRESENTED...

Western history could not be fairly represented without devoting space to the rugged pioneer families who gave impetus to the need for a Western railroad.

Many of the tools and implements necessary to stay alive in that danger area have been retired to the U. P. collection where visitors can examine them and go away with a much better idea of frontier life.

A hugh sauerkraut stomper, a grain flail, a barley fork and a cradle scythe—all hand made and predominately of wood—clearly show the exhausting labor of pioneer living.

"Golden Spike Replica"

EARLY EQUIPMENT...

Union Pacific Railroad equipment improved steadily with the still continuing "age of modern miracles" and left behind many momentoes.

Surveying instruments used by Gen. Grenville M. Dodge, chief engineer of U.P. from May, 1866, to Jan., 1877, are in excellent condition and displayed in glass cases.

Historic spikes and rail sections are being retained as reminders of early construction victories.

And to insure that the countless day-by-day activities of operating the first railroads are not bypassed, the museum has collected miscellaneous items for display, such as ticket punches, badges, telegraph keys, insulators, cable and other equipment, an old locomotive clock, train tickets and schedules, lanterns and many other articles of interest to the general public.

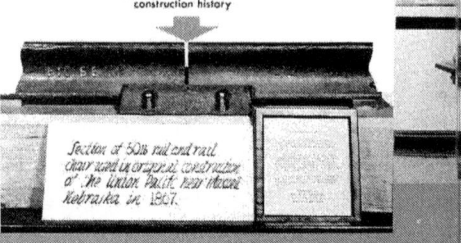
The first rails help trace construction history

Pres. Lincoln's Funeral Car

"... tufts of human hair."

TRIBUTE TO LINCOLN...

Pride of the museum's priceless collection is the display honoring President Abraham Lincoln who, in 1862, signed into law a bill creating the Union Pacific Railroad and authorizing that company to build what was to be the nation's first transcontinental railroad and telegraph line.

Within the museum, the Lincolniana display is considered one of the most complete in the country. A large portion of one wall of the room is entirely taken up by portraits and personal papers of the Civil War president. Among the photographs is one of three known to bear his autograph.

The most prized original document is an executive order which appointed Springer Harbaugh director of the railroad on the a part of the government in October 1863. This particular document is one of the few which he signed "Abraham Lincoln" rather than "A. Lincoln" which became his familiar signature.

In 1864 a private railroad car was built for the president but Lincoln was unable to use it while he lived. This car was then to become his funeral car and a replica of it is another of the Lincoln items on display.

Many of the original furnishing from that car are numbered in the Lincoln collection—a walnut desk, bookcase, a reclining chair, a portion of the silver service, a mirror, four oil paintings and two davenports, one extra long for the president and capable of being converted into a bed.

These items occupied space in Pres. Lincoln's car

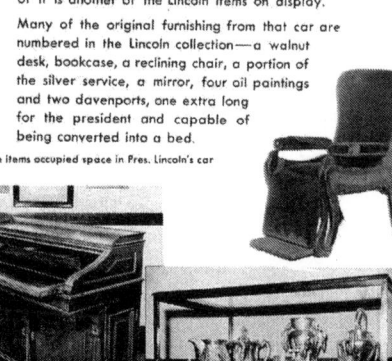

INDIANS...
AN INTEGRAL PART

Like brothers under the same coat, the story of the American Indian goes along with the construction of the nation's Western railroad.

Among the museum's more bizarre items preserved to keep the Indian legend alive is a Shoshone Indian headdress made of wild turkey feathers which trailed to the wearer's ankles. This headdress does not appear unusual until close inspection reveals that each feather is decorated with a tuft of human hair.

Tomahawks, bows and arrows and many items of Indian clothing make up a sizeable display. Each of the articles has a different story behind it.

THE OUTLAW PERIOD...

Synonymous with the difficulties early construction gangs had with the Indians were the string of lesser battles waged against the infamous Western outlaw. The museum has an excellent representation of grim momentoes from that period.

A gun owned by Tom Horn, the "Wyoming Man Killer," and a piece of the rope with which he was hanged tell of the violence surrounding his life.

Another case holds the leg irons used to shackle "Big Nose George" Parrott, another Wyoming desperado, and the top half of his skull. Parrott was executed in frontier fashion for the attempted robbery of a Union Pacific train and the slaying of two posse members who pursued him.

Lesser known criminals are represented by one case that is filled with deadly weapons, all removed from criminals by Union Pacific special agents.

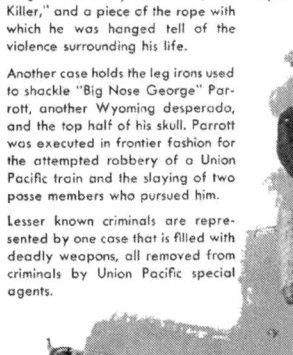

These were the men who opened our great western expanses for settlement. They were the men who faced the dangers and hardships of frontier living.

It is fitting, therefore, that we dedicate this museum to the builders of this railroad and to the early pioneers who opened the great west to colonization. Union Pacific hopes that you will enjoy your visit.

A. E. Stoddard, President
Union Pacific Railroad

Other Points of Interest in OMAHA..

JOSLYN ART MUSEUM — 22nd and Dodge Streets
A $4 million museum, second in per capita attendance in the nation . . . tours arranged.

OMAHA GRAIN EXCHANGE — 19th and Harney Streets
One of the nation's leading grain markets.

OMAHA PUBLIC LIBRARY — 19th and Harney Streets
Houses nearly 250,000 books, a complete assortment of pamphlets, periodicals and newspapers.

MUNICIPAL AUDITORIUM — 17th Street at Capital Ave.
A new, $7 million building, offering attractive accommodations for concerts, conventions, stage productions and other events.

UNION STATION — 10th and Marcy Streets
Thousands of travelers pass through this modern terminal each day.

UNION STOCK YARDS AND LIVESTOCK EXCHANGE BUILDING — 29th and O Streets
More than 100 acres of buildings and paved pens and alleys comprise this world-famed center of Omaha's great livestock industry.

MUNICIPAL STADIUM
13th Street and Bert Murphy Drive
Home of the Triple-A Omaha Cardinals, used also for football games.

RIVERVIEW PARK AND ZOO
13th Street and Deer Park Blvd.
Picnic grounds, playgrounds, a large lagoon and a new zoo.

LEVI CARTER PARK
North on 16th Street and east on Locust Street
Another "summer playground" offering picnic areas, facilities for boating and fishing.

WORLD WAR II MEMORIAL
Dodge Street and Happy Hollow Blvd.
A half-million dollar memorial dedicated to the men and women who gave their lives in service during World War II.

AK-SAR-BEN FIELD AND COLISEUM
63rd and Shirley Streets
Site of the annual racing meet and other events, Ak-Sar-Ben is one of the nation's largest and most active civic organizations.

BOYS TOWN
11 miles west of Omaha on Dodge Street — Highway 30
Father Flanagan's world-famous home for boys, a thriving community within itself. Guides on duty.

UNION PACIFIC RAILROAD

UNION PACIFIC HISTORICAL MUSEUM

HEADQUARTERS BUILDING · OMAHA

Just discovered that your May, 1957 issue of
Lincoln Lore was on the Lincoln funeral car;
if you have any copies left will you please
send me one. Illinois State Historical sent
me a thermofaxed copy, but not too clear.
According to them the car was destroyed by
fire--man at Lancaster, Mo supposed to have
owned "Lincoln car" after turn of century!
Now I wonder!

          Carl Landrum
          920 Spring St
          Quincy, Illinois

LL 1431
Sent 2-16-65

Dr R G McMurtry
Lincoln National Life Foundation
Fort Wayne, Indiana

1285 Albion Street, Apt. 108
Denver 20, Colorado
December 1, 1959

Dr. Gerald R. McMurtry
Director, Lincoln National Life Foundation
1301 South Harrison
Fort Wayne 1
Indiana

Dear Sir:

    Dr. Wayne Grover, United States Archivist suggested that I write you, as you might be able to advise me of pertinent articles that might have appeared in newspapers in 1865, before the death of President Lincoln, relating to the oil panels (paintings) which hung in the private railroad car of Abraham Lincoln.

    According to authentic information, the car was built in 1863-64 in the U. S. Military car shops, Alexandria, Va. The panels however, eight in number, were not hung in the car until 1865, and they were placed there in Washington, D. C. The panels, presumably hung between the windows of the car, possibly in the front compartment (the reception room) and the back one (the general sitting room.) The middle compartment was Lincoln's state-room. These panels were representative of America, its growth, etc.

    John D. Howland, known also as Captain John D. Howland, although the Captain was honorary, given to him in the Indian Wars, often told my sister and myself that he had painted the panels for Abraham Lincoln's private car. There was also a clipping, but this has long since disappeared. As I remember, however, it verified his statement. My father, this artist, has been dead forty-five years, but I have never forgotten his words. He was an extremely honorable man, there would be no reason to doubt him; especially as in 95 years, apparently no one has ever disputed as to the painter.

    In 1865, J. D. Howland, also spoken of as Jack Howland, and Johnny Howland left Colorado by wagon train bound for Washington, D. C. presumably to hang his panels in the Lincoln car. He was then not quite 22 years old, but was known to everyone in the Territory as an artist. Newspapers of that day in Colorado mentioned his paintings frequently. How he came to be commissioned to paint the panels I do not know, but I have thought, that they might have been a gift to the President, by Colorado Territory to be hung in his car.

    It seems to me mention must have been made of this in newspapers of that day, which as I said before may have a few lines relating to the pertinent information needed.

Re: J. D. Howland
Panels Abraham Lincoln Car

-2-

These panels were taken from the car in 1898 at the Trans-Mississippi Exposition at Omaha, or at any rate before 1903 when it was sold to Mr. Snow. The car was destroyed by fire in Minnesota, some years later.

The Joslyn Museum at Omaha owns four of the original panels; the Union Pacific Museum, also of Omaha, has four of them. I have seen them and been furnished with photographs for my work, which is a Biography of J. D. Howland, now nearing completion. Both Museums are deeply interested in my studies.

Specifically, the time that is important to consider is March 1, 1865 to the date of the President's death, in formulating the period when young Howland would have arrived from the Territories. Any papers from Colorado Territory which would appertain to this, of course could have been as early as the last half of 1864, at which time, Oct. 8, Howland received his discharge from the 1st Colorado Volunteer Regiment, and started to organize a wagon train bound for the states, for U. S. Marshall Hunt. Howland was Captain of this train and accompanied it to the River.

I shall appreciate any suggestions or even the slightest information that could be documented and tie up with my knowledge and findings.

Very sincerely,

Kate Howland Charles
(Mrs) Kate Howland Charles

KHC/pm
cc

December 10, 1959

Mrs. Kate Howland Charles
1285 Albion Street
Apartment 108
Denver 20, Colorado

Dear Mrs. Charles:

I have your letter of December 1 relative to the all painted panels which hung in the Lincoln funeral car. In order to give you what information I have regarding the Lincoln funeral car I am enclosing with this letter Lincoln Lore No. 1431 dated May 1957. On page 4 you will find some mention made of the wooden panels that were hand painted depicting landscape scenes.

Since writing this article I have acquired what I believe to be two of the original panels from the Lincoln funeral train. They measure $12\frac{1}{4}$ inches by 15 inches. One painting depicts a woodland scene with a house and the other painting depicts a man sharping a tool on a grindstone. I have reason to feel that these are authentic panels. I have pretty good information regarding them to cause me to believe that they are authentic.

I have not heard of the name of John D. Howland as having had any connection with the building or the decoration of the Lincoln funeral car.

I regret very much that I am unable to provide you with the information you need regarding John D. Howland.

Sincerely,

RGMcMurtry:dh   Director

Buffalo and Erie County Historical Society   Founded 1862
25 Nottingham Court · BUFFALO · New York 14216   716-TR3-9644

December 23, 1964

Mr. R. Gerald McMurtry, Director
The Lincoln National Life Foundation
1301 South Harrison St.
Fort Wayne, Indiana

Dear Mr. McMurtry:

In response to your letter of December 18, 1964 ordering a photograph of the Lincoln funeral procession in Buffalo, I am sending you a list of all the Lincoln funeral photographs which we possess.

A copy of the photograph you requested is on order and will be mailed to you as soon as it is processed. We request that mention be made of the location of the original print if the photograph is added to your files. If you are interested in any of the other Lincoln photographs, we would be happy to supply you with copies of them.

I am enclosing a copy of our photoduplication order form and price list for your information. The Society charges $2.00 for an 8 x 10 glossy print.

Perhaps you can be of assistance to us on a matter concerning President Lincoln. Recently we discovered in our collections a handbill for the Friday evening, April 14th, 1865 performance of "Our American Cousin" at Ford's Theatre. The handbill is mounted and has a notation at the bottom which reads "the above Bill was found in the Box President Lincoln occupied the night of his Assassination at Washington, D.C. Presented by E. A. Fuller." We would like to know how common handbills from that performance are and whether you know of any bills which have been substantiated as being from Lincoln's box that evening. We are attempting to determine the authenticity of this handbill and would appreciate any assistance you can give us.

Sincerely yours,

Anne M. Serio

Anne M. Serio, Curator of Iconography

AMS-j

DANIEL B. NIEDERLANDER	CHARLES CARY	WALTER McCAUSLAND	OWEN B. AUGSPURGER	ROBERT L. WILSON	WALTER S. DUNN, JR.
PRESIDENT	VICE-PRESIDENT	VICE-PRESIDENT	SECRETARY	TREASURER	DIRECTOR

Photographs of Lincoln Funeral Procession in Buffalo, N.Y., April 27, 1865

1. Funeral car used in Buffalo - Caption on photograph reads - "The Funeral Car - used upon the occasion of the Funeral Obsequies of President Lincoln, in Buffalo, N.Y. April 19, and at the Reception of his Remains, April 27, 1865."

2. East Side of Main Street Draped in Mourning for President Lincoln. Does not show the procession.

3. Procession on Main Street looking southwest from Eagle. The hearse is approaching the St. James Hall, corner Main and Eagle Streets, which is not visible in the photograph. Photograph taken by H. L. Bliss.

4. Procession with mounted troops, wagons and the hearse at a halt. There is a large American flag visible in the foreground.

5. Procession with military escort in foreground. The photograph was taken by Louis Brush from the window of Pond & Hambleton's Photograph Gallery, on the west side of Main Street, between Swan and Seneca Streets, looking northeast and showing the Military escort to the catafalque passing the block between Swan and South Division Streets.

December 28, 1964

Miss Anne M. Serio
Curator of Iconography
Buffalo and Erie County Historical Society
25 Nottingham Court
Buffalo, New York 14216

Dear Miss Serio:

       I have your letter of December 23rd relative to the photographs of Lincoln's Funeral which are located in the Buffalo and Erie County Historical Society.

       We will wish to purchase all five of the Lincoln Funeral photographs at $2.00 each, (8 X 10 glossy). Please find enclosed the order form. Upon receipt of your invoice we will remit immediately.

       You have inquired about Ford Theatre playbills for April 14, 1865. Originals are quite valuable and rare. Unfortunately, there are a great many reprints. In 1937 there was privately printed Walter C. Brenner's brochure "The Ford Theatre Lincoln Assassination Playbills". The edition was limited to 75 copies. You should consult this work to determine if you have a genuine item. Perhaps you could secure a copy from the Theatre Collection of the Harvard Library on inter-library loan.

       Yours sincerely,

       R. Gerald McMurtry

RGM/bcs
P.S. I would question the statement that your Ford's Theatre handbill is from Lincoln's box. The name E. A. Fuller is not familiar to me as one of those present at the theatre that evening.

       R. G. M.

the coach lincoln refused to use

By Dr. R. Gerald McMurtry
Director, Lincoln National Life Foundation

THE railway car, which carried President Abraham Lincoln's remains from Washington, D.C., to Springfield, Illinois in the spring of 1865, was considered a triumph of the car builder's art. On the 1,662 mile funeral route approximately two million people saw and admired this beautiful railway coach. However, it had not been designed originally as a funeral car, but as a private presidential car for the Chief Executive. It was thought that a special railway car for Lincoln's own personal use would be efficient for the conduct of the affairs of his office.

The armored car, as originally constructed, was forty-two feet long and eight and one-half feet wide. It was built at the United States Military Car Shops at Alexandria, Virginia. The luxurious interior of the car marked a distinct advance in railway coach comfort.

Evidently, Lincoln preferred not to travel in an armored car of luxurious appointments. Certain newspapers of New York took up the matter of the "Presidential Car" and were ready to chide Lincoln for such pretentiousness. Once the coach was completed, he steadfastly refused to accept the car or to ride in it during his lifetime.

With the assassination and death of Lincoln, the officers in charge of the military car shops were ordered to strip out a portion of the interior of the President's car to provide a suitable funeral coach. With the exterior suitably draped with broadcloth and silver fringe, the car was made ready on April 21, to carry the remains of the President to Springfield, Illinois.

The train of which the funeral car was a part traveled by way of Baltimore, Harrisburg, Philadelphia, Jersey City, New York, Albany, Buffalo, Cleveland, Columbus, Indianapolis and Chicago, arriving on May 3 at the Illinois Capital.

The coach, from time to time, was placed on exhibit. Later, it was used as a railroad work car and in its dilapidated condition was burned beyond any hope of reclamation in the railway yards in Minneapolis, Minnesota on March 18, 1911, when it was enveloped in flames resulting from a grass fire.

Historical News Letter

VOLUME XXX   January 1978   NUMBER 7
Lincoln, Nebraska 68508   Tel. 432-2793

The President Abraham Lincoln Railway Coach, designed especially for Lincoln and completed only a short time before his 1865 assassination, was first used as a funeral coach to carry the President's body from Washington, DC, to Springfield, Illinois. Purchased by the Union Pacific Railroad in 1866, the car was used in various capacities and exhibited in Nebraska and around the country before it was accidentally destroyed by fire in Minneapolis in 1911. The Nebraska State Historical Society owns a window sash taken from the car during one of its several refittings, and the UP Museum in Omaha has other effects.

HISTORICAL ACTIVITIES

The thirty-ninth annual meeting of the January 12th 1888 Blizzard Club was held January 7 in Lincoln. Special guest was Lincoln businessman Max Meyer, 96, one of the few remaining survivors of the legendary 1888 storm. Many others who attended were descendants of survivors. Officers elected at the gathering: William Wood, Lincoln, president; Ellsworth Shromsher, Fremont, vice president; Ann Quinlan, Lincoln, secretary; Irene Woodburn, Lincoln, treasurer; Doris Jenkins, Lincoln, historian.

The Nemaha Valley Museum at Auburn would like to acquire several especially designed display cases to exhibit items from its collection. Each case features a display area for related supplies, glass front, hidden display lights, and full-length door for convenient access. Memorials or donations would be welcomed. . . . Each Tuesday night has been designated volunteer work night at the museum. Although great improvements were made on the museum building in 1977, many details still need attention.

Balt. Sunday Sun
11/9/80

I REMEMBER

Re-enacting Lincoln's Funeral Journey

By ALLEN R. BROUGHAM, JR.

NEARLY 25 years ago I participated in a network television program; the segment, that is, that was broadcast live from Baltimore. I played the part of a bugle boy, though I couldn't play a bugle then and still can't.

It was on Sunday, February 12, 1956, Lincoln's birthday. NBC's "Wide, Wide World" series was presenting a tribute to Lincoln and the Baltimore segment was the re-creation of the arrival of the murdered president's funeral train in Camden Station in 1865 as the first stop of the journey from Washington to Springfield, Ill.

Officials of NBC had asked for a detachment from the 175th Infantry Regiment of the Maryland National Guard to pose in Union uniforms as an honor guard meeting the train as it arrived in the station.

But they didn't reckon with history. I still have clippings from The Sun pertaining to the denial of NBC's request. Col. Roger Whiteford, commanding officer of the "Dandy Fifth," was quoted as saying: "I told them it would be out of keeping with our history and tradition."

Colonel Whiteford explained that the 175th Regiment's dress uniforms were Confederate gray. NBC officials offered to find some Yankee blue uniforms in New York, whereupon the colonel replied that though Maryland was regarded as neutral during the Civil War, a good many of the regiment's men went to Virginia and fought as 1st and 2d Maryland Regiments for the Confederacy.

It was out of the question for any of his men to wear Yankee uniforms, Colonel Whiteford told NBC with finality.

What then happened was that sailors

Mr. Brougham

were put into Union uniforms to act as the honor guard.

My father, a lieutenant commander, was executive officer of the Naval Reserve Training Center at Fort McHenry and he volunteered 25 of his sailors. "After all, we weren't all Johnny Rebs down here during the War Between the States," he was quoted in one of the newspaper stories at the time. "We will be more than proud to have our boys wearing the Union blue tomorrow afternoon."

He also volunteered me to be the bugle boy. I was 15, a student at Hereford High School in northern Baltimore county.

On Saturday, February 11, we rehearsed most of the afternoon. Directors and cameramen from WBAL-TV, then and now the NBC affiliate here, were there on

Continued on Page 33

WBAL's camera awaits the "Lincoln funeral train" at Camden Station.

Rain or shine London Fog® gives the protection you need, the classic style you want!

Forecast: cold, wet winter ahead! Stay dry, stay healthy and look your best in a London Fog® any-weather coat. Shown from our huge collection: the Andes. Single breasted, fly front with split raglan sleeves. Warm zip-out pile liner. No-wrinkle Fortrel® polyester and cotton shell machine washes. Natural for regulars, shorts, longs, ex. long. Sizes 36-46 reg., 36-44 short, 38-46 long, 40-46 ex. long. 97.50 Size 48 & 50, Reg., long, ex.-long. $111

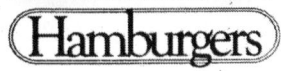

Charles Center York Road Westview Reisterstown Plaza Eastpoint Harundale Golden Ring Timonium Annapolis Mall Salisbury Mall Lancaster Park City In Delaware: 300 Delaware Avenue Concord Mall Christiana Mall

Steam engine, dating to 1856, was borrowed from B. & O.'s Railroad Museum.

Honor guard soldiers were actually sailors from Naval Reserve at Fort McHenry.

Lincoln's Funeral Journey

Continued from 31

the Camden Station platform telling us all what to do.

Besides the honor guard, those meeting the B. & O. Railroad funeral train were local "dignitaries." They weren't representing any particular Baltimoreans, such as the mayor and other prominent persons, but were men and women in costumes of the times. The dignitaries were played by B & O. employee volunteers.

Over and over, the train—a locomotive, boxcar and two coaches—backed out of the station and then pulled in to a stop on Track 2, and then we all went through our paces. My part was to carry a bugle and walk behind the casket that soldiers were carrying from the baggage car.

The engine, the William Mason, black smoke belching from its wide, funnel-shaped stack, was from the B. & O.'s Mount Clare Railroad Museum. It was built in 1856 and was a twin of the one that pulled Lincoln's last train.

Though the train and costumes were authentic for the year 1865, the American flags on the engine were not. The flags contained 48 stars, which was proper for 1956. However, the flags were kept partially furled so that only a few stars showed. The flag in April, 1865, carried 35 stars. A 36th star, for Nevada, was added in July.

On Sunday, we rehearsed again from about 10 a.m. until noon, then had to report back at 4 p.m. We were served coffee and box lunches from a buffet car on an adjacent track.

All of the segments in "Wide, Wide World" were live, with Dave Garroway in New York the anchorman. My father was not one of the soldiers, but he stood next to one of the cameramen who was on a dais on the station platform.

Our segment was broadcast sometime close to 5 o'clock. The train puffed into the station for the last time, its big bell tolling. As muffled drums beat, soldiers carried the casket from the baggage car and the dignitaries fell in behind, some of them having been directed to pretend to be crying.

It took less than 3 minutes and my father and I have never seen it. I wish WBAL had borrowed a copy of the film to show the participants.

When I was 30, I went to work for the B & O. and am now tower operator at Halethorpe.

Today

Lincoln and railroads

And how a retired painter combined an unusual hobby with some interesting tales

By RITA TRUSCHEL
Gazette Staff Writer

LEWISTON — Frank Cornell, 71, has been a self-confessed "railroad nut" for 65 years, and a "Lincoln nut" for almost as long. Today — 172 years after the birth of Abraham Lincoln — Cornell recalls how he combined both passions.

For the past 12 years, he has tried to learn as much as possible about the rail car that carried Lincoln's body to Springfield, Ill.

It is a rare hobby for a retired sign painter. But after unearthing, in no particular order, a small flood of facts and figures about the car, Cornell says, "It will take another 10 years at least" before his interest flags.

Cornell's interest began with another assassination, that of Robert Kennedy. He was watching the progress of Kennedy's funeral train on television, and wondered what happened to Lincoln's funeral car.

"It took me almost two months to find my first picture," he said. Since then, he has built up a network of contacts among historians and librarians across the country and receives a regular stream of correspondence.

Cornell, of 4555 Creek Road, will give a slide show and lecture on Lincoln's funeral car at 6 p.m. Feb. 26 at First Baptist Church in Niagara Falls.

Among the facts he reveals is that, although the rail car was built by a group of master carpenters especially for Lincoln's use during his lifetime, the president never saw it.

"He never wanted it," Cornell said. "It was too rich for his blood."

The car took two years to outfit, from 1863 to 1865. Lincoln was assassinated on April 14, 1865.

The car, which never served the purpose for which it was built, was altered to convey the bodies of the fallen president and his dead son, Willie, whose body was exhumed from a Washington cemetery, back to their final resting places in Illinois.

At this point, Cornell considers the story of the rail car to be intertwined with that of Myron Lamson of Onondaga County in New York. Lamson, a mechanic on the Baltimore and Ohio Railroad, did the interior alterations, removing furniture and railings,

from the car that carried the coffins home.

Afterward, the car, which cost $6,000 to build, was sold to the Union Pacific Railroad for $6,840, where it was used for many years. But Lamson apparently retained his interest in it, too. In 1908, to

celebrate the 42nd encampment of the Grand Army of the Republic in Toledo, Ohio, Lamson, now a prosperous merchant, printed 300,000 souvenir postcards picturing the Lincoln car the day after alterations were complete.

NIAGARA GAZETTE

Thursday, February 12, 1981

Ann Landers	2	
Erma Bombeck	6	
Bridge	5	
To Your Health	6	

...Post Card...

ON the 19th of April, 1865, (exactly four years from the surrender of Fort Sumter) when even hope had fled, and a day later passed away, Lincoln was shot and a day later passed away. The nation was plunged into mourning. The car of illustration on the reverse side was built by the President of the U.S. and his Cabinet. It became his funeral car, and on April 21st, 1865, after most impressive obsequies, this car, flowing the President's remains, was attached to the locomotive "Old Nashville," heavily draped with black, slowly moved out of Washington amid a vast concourse of silent and sad spectators. History does not record another such spectacle as the passing of this funeral train through the most populous sections of the Union. At every public place along the route vast throngs stood with uncovered heads while the train passed by. In city and country alike, buildings were draped in mourning and flags flew at half mast. The day the train reached Springfield, Ill., and on the following day, as a closing scene, "Peace Troubled Soul," the casket was closed forever. Mr. Lamson, the father of the Lamson Brothers, an eminent mechanic served on a committee during the construction of this car and did the remodeling. The photograph here seen is the family's for 43 years; now that a united nation and everything connected with his life and death, no thought it appropriate that we should present this picture to be held for whom our union is so grandly indebted.

THE LAMSON BROTHERS COMPANY, Toledo, Ohio.

Copyrighted, 1908.

(FOR ADDRESS ONLY)

Frank Cornell, left, of Lewiston has spent 12 years investigating the history of the railroad car, above, that bore Lincoln's body to his grave. Among his memorabilia is a postcard issued in 1908 picturing the vehicle.

The postcards are now a rarity, according to Cornell. The rail car itself burned on March 15, 1911. "All that's left is a piece of the car made into a desk for a coach at the University of Minnesota," Cornell said.

Mr. Mark Neely,Jr.
Louis A. Warren
Lincoln Library
and Museum
Fort Wayne,Indiana   Monday
46801   August 13,1982

Dear Mark,

    Herewith is something that I've been accumulating for you for several months.So,today I made up my mind it had to go. To me it is so very interesting and I do so much hope you like it. It is just anoffbeat thing about the Lincoln Railroad Funeral Car. I assume that you know all about this postecard?

    Over the thirteen years I've been beating my mind out searching for this Lincoln Car material all I've been able to accumulate is six of these card. I've a few of the later reprints too. I've paid $2.00/$7.50/$10.00/$12.50/$15.00/$17/50 for them. One I just obtain-last month at a Flea Market in Adamston,Penn......Amish Country. I'll be running an ad one of these days looking for more.

    I've only one with a stamp on it (Photo)mailed from Toledo in 1908. I'd like several more. Can you imagine #300,000 printed and they are so scarce? I only know of three others with a stamp on them. Does your museum have any.....how many?

    Once again....you probably figured that that Cornell Fellow had given up the Lincoln Car Chase. No way...I'll never give up. As a matter of fact I'm thinking of puttin' on a big push this Winter. I've a very excellent batch of excellent leads.

    Do you get and read the CIVIL WAR TIMES. Did you see my item in the Mail Call in July Issue? I've had six people call me and write about the Lincoln Car. Two were very very good and helped a bit.

    A lady from Denver sent me a clipping telling about when the enterior of the Lincoln was torn out in 1870 when they enstalled passenger seats to use it between Denver and Golden on the Colorado Central.The carpenter took some of the hard wood home and made two inlaid chests. There are two chest in the picture. I'm going to try and get a better photo all this one isn't too bad.

The only other piece of the Llcoln Car proper is a small silver of the wooden window from a physical ed teacher has at the University of Minneasota. He made it into a tie clasp. I have a letter from him and a sketch.

Also, I located a brass bell in the Mad River Railroad Museum near Toledo who have the bell from the Nashville hauling engine......Cleveland to Columbus.

When I get it organized I will send you an article of all the whys and whos about the Lincoln Car construction. Why was it built and who financed it? It is not a bit like what you might think. Historians have never come up with anything that made any sense. You can judge for yourself.

For awhile lately I was sort of thinking my wife was about to box up all thse Lincoln Car stuff and ship it to you. I was in bad bad shape. I could hardly navigate. I was a mess.....stiff all over.....ache from head to toe. My pains had me believing the man upstairs wanted me.

I went to the ol' saw bones in the village. He sent me to the hospital lab and they took a mess of blood and urine out of me. Waiting for the report had me fretting. I had a friend who had the same symtoms. They found him dead at 57 settlng on the John one day.

But, my report......no sugar....clear urine...and my cloistral was normal....my blood pressure a bit high..... blood cance check clear. So what was wrong? How I love my roast beef...ham...chops...hot dogs...hamburgers...milk aggs etc. No more...veal only....skim milk...one slice of grain bread a day....fruit and vegetables galore.....and cereals like shredded wheat and oatmeal...no sugar. Man! A diet like that will starve a man to death. But, I'm still here. Lost about eight pounds.

The big problem those pills. They kill me. I cut them in half.....skipped days and they still make me sleepy and dizzy......my head swims. I drink a sip of milk when I take them and that helps a bit. Take them before I go to bed and I wake up with my head swimming.

Well, that is enough for this time, I hope you like my postcard research effort, I am

```
************************
** Lincoln Car Chaser **
************************
```

FRANK W. CORNELL
4955 Creek Road
LEWISTON, NEW YORK
14092

THE
***

ABRAHAM LINCOLN
****

RAILROAD FUNERAL CAR   by FRANK W.CORNELL
********************   *******************

POSTECARD......1908
****

Myron Hawley Lamson was born in Terry Hollow, near Cedar-
ville in Onondaga County, New York on the 25th of February
in 1823. He was the son of Sterling and Olive (Crocker)
Lamson.

Myron, grew up and settled in the Village of Elbridge near
by and married Laura the daughter of the proprietor of the
local hotel. By trade he was a master wagon and carriage
maker.......and a skilled blacksmith.

Little did he know that the fickle finger of fate had him
tagged to fill a niche in the future History of the United
States. Small for sure but well worth its significant rem-
memberance.

****

In early November of 1863 a group of master railroad car
builders were beset with the task of constructing an ornate
luxuruios for its day salon railroad car.....in the car shop
inside the military stockade of the United States Military
Railroad Command of the Orange, Alexandria & Manassa Gap
Railroad in Alexandria, Virginia. It was destined for the
private use of the 16th President of the United States....
Abraham Lincoln.

In Mid-February of 1865, the elegant railroad car was comp-
pleted. Lincoln made several appointments to inspect it but
never kept a one. He never ever laid live eyes upon it. He
never rode in it except in death. Abe Lincoln never cared
for elegance......the car it seemed was to rich for his
blood. Besides he alread had a railroad car supplied by the
Military Railroad Command.

****

On April 14th 1865 when John Wilkes Booth fired the fatal
shot that snuffed out the life of Abraham Lincoln in Ford's
Theatre the Lincoln Car stood idly by on a siding of the
Orange, Alexandrie & Manassa Gap Railroad across the Potomac
River in Alexandria, Virginia.

It was a white elephant. Nobody wanted it. It was just so much Civil War junk. In all probability it would of been sold at auction to the highest bidder. But the mist of fate had another use for it. It too would take its place in the annals of history.

****

And fate did intercede. No sooner had Sec. of War Stanton uttered those immortal words "Now He Belongs to the Ages" than a master plan sprung into existance for a massive state funeral. The Lincoln Car was to be the centerpiece of the most elegant railroad funeral cortege that would ever take place in the United States.

Muffled drums hammered the dirge of death. And the multitudes did weep. Cannon would roar like thunder. Flowers would strew its path. It would be viewed in its glory as it bore the martyred remains of Abe Lincoln 1662 miles in a "Long Sad Journey",back to the praires of Illinois.

****

At that time,Myron Lamson,at age 43 was a sergent,an enlisted railroad mechanic in the service of the Baltimore & Ohio Railroad in Washington,D.C. He was sent across the Potomac to Alexandria to alter the Lincoln Car into a railroad funeral hearse. All unneeded furniture was placed in storage. And a catafalgue was built in the State Room for the coffin to rest upon. The solid brass railing was removed to facilitate the moving of the casket in and out of the carat the ten cities enroute where it would be placed in mourning. In the salon room a place was made to carry casket of Willie Lincoln whose remains had been exhumed. He would go home to Springfield with his dad.

The car was decorated in mourning.....bedecked in black satin drapping,silver fringe and tassles. For the next fourteen days it would be the .....April 21st to May 3rd.....the focal point of sorrow.....never to be forgotten. Lamson did dot drape the Lincoln Car. That was done by a man named Alexander.

Lamson,his work completed called in a professional photographer,supposedly Matthew Brady and had a picture taken. He is on the rear platform in Civil War Sergent Uniform.

****

Lamson as a member of the Sergent Guard de Les Invalid accomped the Lincoln Caroll the way to Springfield. He stood vigil over the car and Lincolns remains. In all probabliity he took part in the funeral cortege in Springfield.

At the conclusion of the Civil War, mustered out he returned home to Elbridge in Onondaga County, New York. In 1867-69 he was elected president of the village....he served three terms.

Lamson had a daughter and three sons. The sons heeded Horace Greely "Go West Young Men, Go West!" They settled in Toledo, Ohio. They became engaged in a successful department store business.....Lamson Brothers of Toledo. In 1888, Lamson with his wife and daughter joined them.

In August of 1908, the Grand Army of the Republic, the Civil War Veterans, gathered for their 42nd Encampment in Toledo, Ohio. As a gesture of patriotism and complete envolvement the Lamson Family dug out the old picture of Abraham Lincoln Railroad Funeral Car. They had 300,000 picture souvenir postcards printed. Ads were placed in the Toledo Blade Newspaper offerthem free to the veterans and their friends.....the public in general.

****

The picture of the Lincoln Car is on the front of the car. An oval ornate frame is above the car with the words "The Lincoln Funeral Car.....Souvenir 42nd Encampment G.A.R. At the left is a bust of Lincoln. Half of the rear of the postcard is printed a description of the car.

The cards is not only a historical Lincoln item, but postcard collectable and a philatelic gem with a stamp on it mailed from Toledo in August of 1908.

****

Now, 300,000 postcards is an awful lot of postcards. That was seventy three years ago at the time this was written.....l981. Today they are few and far between. Recently while at Adamston, Pennsy in Amish Land I was able to purchase one for $17.50.

One with a stamp on it usually brings about $20.00 in superb condition. One with a stamp affixed and mailed from Toledo with 1908 cancellation could bring $100. That would depend just on how bad the buyer wanted it.

Over a period of thirteen years I,ve only seen three with a stamp affixed. Constantly on the allert for these cardsall I have been able to come by is six. I have had several chances to sell them but "No Way" will i part with them. Actually I'm still searching for them, ready and willing to buy.

****

That for what it is worth is the tale of the Abraham Lincoln Railroad Funeral Car. Right or wrong it stands to be corrected and added too. Be my guest.

What happened to the Abraham Lincoln Railroad Car? That is a long story. Sad, but it was destroyed in a raging praire grass fire at Columbia Heights in Minneapolis, Minnesota on March 15th, Wednesday, 1908.

The research for this story was done by Frank W. Cornell of 4955 Creek Road, Lewiston, New York 14092 (716) 754-7026. For the past twelve years (1981) the tracks of the historical old railroad vehicle have been haunted. You would have to see the vast accumulation of old pictures and related material to really appreciate it. There still a dozen real evasive puzzling items about the Lincoln Car to be found. Not satisfied.....I just keep bungling on in hope that somewhere I'll find it. You'd be surprised how it has happened and will happen again. That is the fun of it all.

Frank W. Cornell

FRANK W. CORNELL
4955 Creek Road
Lewiston, New York   14092

****
* The LINCOLN CAR CHASER *
****

* a little something extra was brought to my attention in a letter from Toledo, Ohio. The Lamson Brothers of Toledo after an 94 years in business folded. The department store building still in existance and modernized still carries on.

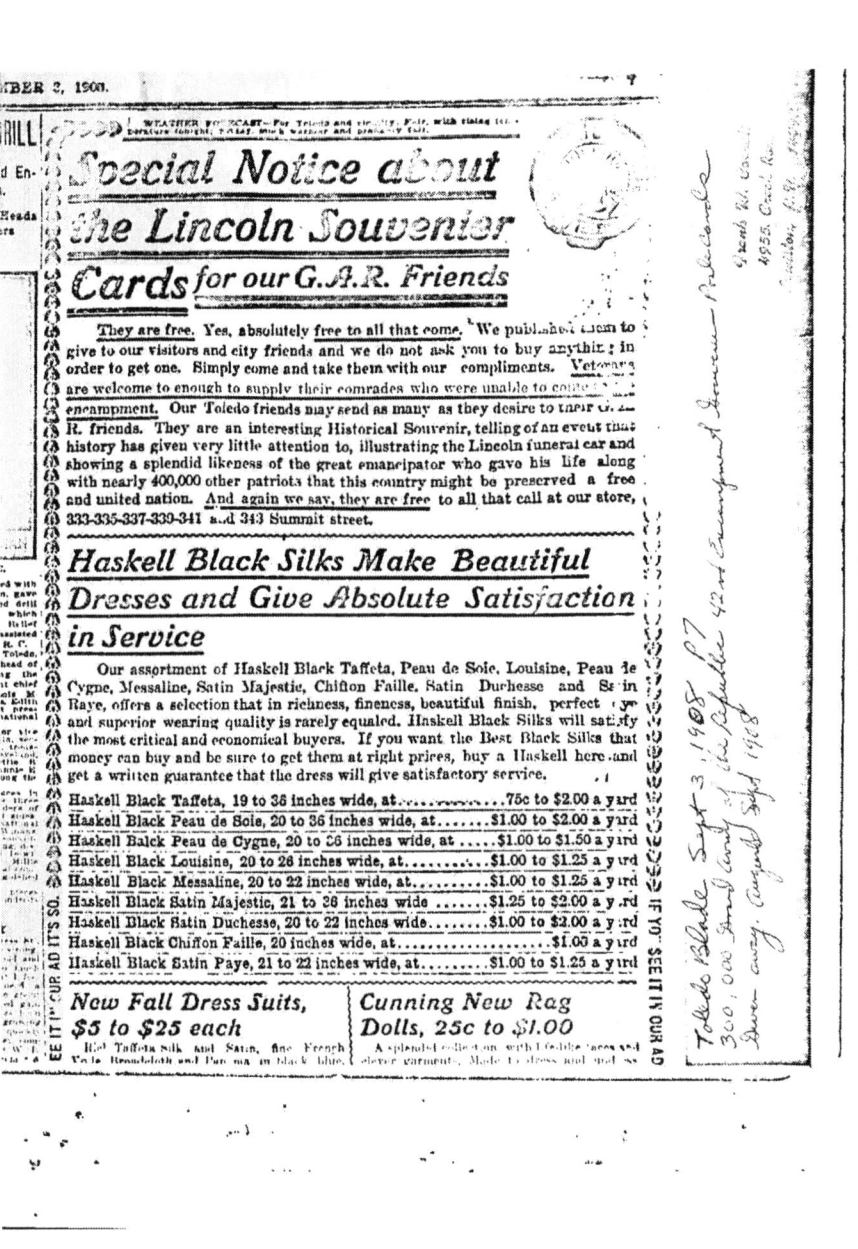

Special Notice about the Lincoln Souvenier Cards for our G.A.R. Friends

They are free. Yes, absolutely free to all that come. We publish them to give to our visitors and city friends and we do not ask you to buy anything in order to get one. Simply come and take them with our compliments. Veterans are welcome to enough to supply their comrades who were unable to come to encampment. Our Toledo friends may send as many as they desire to their G. A. R. friends. They are an interesting Historical Souvenir, telling of an event that history has given very little attention to, illustrating the Lincoln funeral car and showing a splendid likeness of the great emancipator who gave his life along with nearly 400,000 other patriots that this country might be preserved a free and united nation. And again we say, they are free to all that call at our store, 333-335-337-339-341 and 343 Summit street.

Haskell Black Silks Make Beautiful Dresses and Give Absolute Satisfaction in Service

Our assortment of Haskell Black Taffeta, Peau de Soie, Louisine, Peau de Cygne, Messaline, Satin Majestic, Chiffon Faille, Satin Duchesse and Satin Raye, offers a selection that in richness, fineness, beautiful finish, perfect dye and superior wearing quality is rarely equaled. Haskell Black Silks will satisfy the most critical and economical buyers. If you want the Best Black Silks that money can buy and be sure to get them at right prices, buy a Haskell here and get a written guarantee that the dress will give satisfactory service.

Haskell Black Taffeta, 19 to 36 inches wide, at . . . . 75c to $2.00 a yard
Haskell Black Peau de Soie, 20 to 36 inches wide, at . . . . $1.00 to $2.00 a yard
Haskell Black Peau de Cygne, 20 to 36 inches wide, at . . . . . $1.00 to $1.50 a yard
Haskell Black Louisine, 20 to 26 inches wide, at . . . . $1.00 to $1.25 a yard
Haskell Black Messaline, 20 to 22 inches wide, at . . . . $1.00 to $1.25 a yard
Haskell Black Satin Majestic, 21 to 26 inches wide . . . . $1.25 to $2.00 a yard
Haskell Black Satin Duchesse, 20 to 22 inches wide . . . . $1.00 to $2.00 a yard
Haskell Black Chiffon Faille, 20 inches wide, at . . . . $1.05 a yard
Haskell Black Satin Paye, 21 to 22 inches wide, at . . . . $1.00 to $1.25 a yard

New Fall Dress Suits, $5 to $25 each

Cunning New Rag Dolls, 25c to $1.00

...Post Card...

ON the 14th of April, 1865, (exactly four years after the surrender of Fort Sumter) when everything looked hopeful and the war was over, President Lincoln was shot and a day later passed away, and the nation was plunged into mourning. The car illustrated on this card had recently been built for the President and his Cabinet. It became his funeral car, and on April 21st, after most impressive obsequies, this car (bearing the President's remains,) with six other cars and the locomotive all heavily draped with black, slowly moved out of Washington amid a vast crowd of silent and sad spectators. History does not record a more touching spectacle than the passing of this funeral train through the most populous states of the Union. At every point along the route vast throngs stood with uncovered heads while the train passed by. In city and country buildings were draped in mourning and flags drooped at half mast. On May 3rd the train reached Springfield, Ill., and on the following day, as a chorus sang "Peace, Troubled Soul," the casket was closed forever. Myron H. Lamson, the father of the Lamson Brothers, an enlisted mechanic, served as assistant foreman during the construction of this car and the remodeling to receive the President's remains. The photograph has been in the family for 43 years and now that a united nation reveres the memory of Lincoln and everything connected with his life and death, we thought it appropriate that we should present this picture to the brave men to whom our nation is so greatly indebted.

THE LAMSON BROTHERS COMPANY
August 31st, 1908.   TOLEDO, OHIO.
COPYRIGHTED, 1908.

Front and rear views of Abraham Lincoln Poste Card. In 1908 the 42nd Encampent of the Grand Army of the Republic was held in August in Toledo, Ohio. There were 300,000 of these cards printed and given away by Lamson's Brothers Department Store as a souvenir of this historical event. They are quite difficult to come by at this time.

The soldier on the front platform is Myron Hawley Lamson who was an enlisted mechanic of the Baltimore &Ohio Railroad. At Alexandria, Virginia he altered the car into a funeral car. He was a Sargent of the Guard de les Invalid whose duty it was to protect the Lincoln Car during the 1662 mile long sad journey.

He had this picture taken supposedly by Matthew Brady. It was in the Lamson Family until used to make these Lincoln Funeral Railroad-Grand Army of the Republic Postcards in 1908.

Lamson Brothers Department of Toledo ceased to exist as of 1980 when the business was ended.

February 22, 1982

Francis W. Cornell
4955 Creek Road
Lewiston, N.Y. 14092

Lincoln Souvenir Cards Free

We want every visitor and every resident of Toledo to have one. Just call at the store any day this week and receive one of these interesting historical souvenirs with our compliments.

The Lamson Brothers Company
333=335=337=339=341=343 Summit Street.

On the 14th day of April, 1865 (exactly four years after the surrender of Fort Sumter), when everything looked hopeful and the war was over, President Lincoln was shot and a day later passed away, and the nation was plunged into mourning. The car illustrated on this card had recently been built for the President and his cabinet. It became his funeral car and on April 21st, after most impressive obsequies, this car (bearing the President's remains), with six other cars and the locomotive all heavily draped with black, slowly moved out of Washington amid a vast crowd of silent and sad spectators. History does not record a more touching spectacle than the passing of this funeral train through the most populous states of the Union. At every point along the route vast throngs stood with uncovered heads while the train passed by. In city and country buildings were draped in mourning and flags drooped at half mast. On May 3rd the train reached Springfield, Ill., and on the following day, as a chorus sang "Peace, Troubled Soul," the casket was closed forever. Myron H. Lamson, the father of the Lamson Brothers, an enlisted mechanic, served as assistant foreman during the construction of this car and the remodeling to receive the President's remains. The photograph has been in the family for 43 years and now that a united nation reveres the memory of Lincoln and everything connected with his life and death, we thought it appropriate that we should present this picture to the brave men to whom our nation is so greatly indebted.

The Lamson Brothers Co.
August 31st, 1908.   Toledo, Ohio.

IF YOU SEE IT IN OUR AD IT'S SO.

This photograph is a copy of the original cropped and touched up picture that belonged to the Myron Hawley Lamson who altered the Abraham Lincoln Railroad Car into a funeral car. Why this was done is a big question. This was not the photo used on the Lincoln Gar Postcarde.

Picture.....courtesy of the University of Delaware Lincoln Collection.

Frank W. Cornell
4955 Creek Road
Lewiston, N.Y. 14092

The Abraham Lincoln Railroad Funeral Car as it was photographed at Buffalo, New York on April 27, 1865 enroute from Washington, D.C. to Springfield, Illinois with the remains of the martyred 16th President of the United States. Aboard also was the small coffin of Willie Lincoln who had died several years ago.

The Lincoln Car was built at Alexandria, Virginia from early November 1863 to Mid-November in the Car Shops of the United States Military Railroad Command on the Orange, Alexandria & Manassa Gap Railroad.

It was made of hard woods by master railroad car builders. It was 42 ft. 6 inches over all and eight ft. six inches high and wide. The four trucks were to provide a comfortable ride. The design was copied from a typical Pennsylvania Railroad Passenger car of the era, The car cost approximately $10,000. A passenger car of that period cost $3,000.

The other car in the picture is the Veep-Car of the Philadelphia, Wilmington and Baltimore Railroad. It was loned for the funeral by that railroad. It was called the "Brass Car" because it carried the brass...military generals etc.

The Civil War Sergent on the rear platform is Myron Hawley Lamson. He was in charge of altering the Lincoln Railroad Car into a Funeral Car for the Baltimore and Ohio Railroad. He was a member of the Sergent Guard de Les Invalid that guard the funeral car during the Long Sad Journey.

The other man is Pinkerton the famous dective.

The Lincoln Car was sold to the Union Pacific Railroad in April of 1866. The elements and railroad usage on the Colorado Central utterly destroyed it. In 1904 a Franklin B. Snow bought it for $6,840 from the Union Pacific and exhibited it at the St. Louis Expo.

In 1905 the Hon. Thomas Lowry paid off mechanics liens on the car and took it to Minneapolis. He was a street car and real estate tycoon. He used the car to attract people to Colombia Heighs....a land developement of his. He tried to give the car to several historical organizations with no takers

On March 15, 1911 the Lincoln Car was completely destroyed in a raging praire grass fire. All that remained was a small piece of a window frame. That piece was made into a tie clasp by a gentleman who was a physical ed instructor at the University of Minneasota.

This is the finest photo of the two cars that is available. The original is in the possession of the Buffalo-Erie County Historical Society.

Courtesy of the Buffalo-Erie County Historical Society.

Frank W. Cornell
4955 Creek Road
Lewiston, N.Y. 14092

This photograph of the Abraham Lincoln Furneral Car was taken on April 20,1865, the day before it was taken across the Potomac to the Baltimore & Ohio Railroad Station to receive the casket of the assinated 16th President of the United States. It suposedly was taken by Matthew Brady. The altering and trimming of the railroad car for the funeral had just then been completed. This is the unaltered photograph from which the Grand Army of the Republic cropped photograph from which the printing plate for the 300,000 printing of the souvenir Lamson Brother's Department was made.

The Civil War Soldier on the rear platform is Myron Hawley Lamson who was an enlisted mechanic in the service of the Baltimore & Ohio Railroad in Washington. It is not visable on this print but that ornate hand-wrought brass railing behind which Lamson is standing has been removed from the other end of the car to facilitate the taking of the casket in and out of the funeral car at the places enroute. He also built a catafalgue in the car upon which the casket rested. Some furniture was also placed in storage. He had nothing to do with the trimming of the car. That was done by a man named Alexandria Jr.,

This photograph was taken in front of the car shop that can be seen at the right. It was in these car shops inside the stockade of the United States Military Command of the Orange, Alexandria & Manassa Gap Railroad in Alexandria, Virginia that the car was built from early November of 1863 to Mid-February of 1865. It was 42 ft 6 inches long and 8½ ft. x 8½ ft wide and high. It cost just about $10,000

After the funeral it was returned to Washington where is was such a task to keep it from being vandalized it was sold to the Union Pacific Railroad for $6,480. It was used as a veep-car for Thomas Durant and Sidney Dillon the officials of the company.

Lamson was a member of the Sargent Guard des les Invalids whose duty it was to guard the Lincoln Car during the long sad journey.

Note the four trucks on the car. This was reasoned to make for a smoother ride. But it proved otherwise jumping the stud switches quite often. The trucks were made by the Union Tyre & Wheel Company of Jersey City under the Patent of W.W.Snow. The trucks were cast in Wilmington of bursted Civil War Cannon by the Lubbock Co. They also, patented the chilled cast iron wheels.

The Lincoln was totally destroyed in a raging praire grass fire at Columbis Heights up in Minneapolis on March 15,1911.

This Photo.......Courtesy of Illinois State Historical Museum
       Courtesy of Lincoln National Life

Friday June 7, 1907

TOLEDO DAILY BLADE, FRIDAY, JUNE 7

CHARGE MADE BY LAWYER

From Page One.

regular talesman of the not sitting on a jury at a familiar figure among professional jurors. Thatcher intimates the nature of what was handed in Friday. The juror gave his name incident to Prosecutor. He denied anything

followed closely upon the of perjury against one season. Today the court this would be sifted, so Thatcher made the pro court that Charles Idolph, owner of the saloon in Barnes' head on the and to have caused the ch he was charged in jury, had held meetings agents of the company, trial he was giving testimony different from that which previous trial before

the defense demanded rate, and yesterday afternoon placed upon the stand of Findlay, a cousin of in the latter, in his testimony had gone to Findlay to to the settlement of and denied knowledge of such he as McKinnis was and had notice of such between them which he in Findlay. They were at an hour at the time fixed by the prosecution down McKinnis ex— he went to Findlay at let witness be conferred of officials testimony was admitted. Thatcher to state demanded to prove. The to charged McKinnis

of that he should not be influenced on the part of himself but said that he had made money asking no questions at all I Smith, occupied a J. A Herrington, of the witness, McKinnis. He also further evidence.

He signed something

FORGET

WE ARE

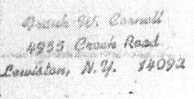

GREEN CORN
WAX BEANS
GREEN PEAS
MUSHROOMS
WATER MELONS
CANTALOUPES
SWEET CHERRIES
HUCKLEBERRIES
GRAPE FRUIT
BROILERS ROASTERS YEARLINGS

F. C. BISHOP & CO.
515 ADAMS ST.
PHONES—Home 7906-7908. Bell 617.

any intention of prosecuting the inquiry farther, but he said that he would investigate the charges as to McKinnis' testimony, which, in his opinion, amounts to a charge of perjury and subornation of perjury. Colonel J. A. Bope, of Findlay, and Harold Fraser, counsel for the company, have personally requested that the matter be sifted to the bottom.

Attorney Thatcher has likewise demanded a full investigation of the McKinnis matter, and has asked that Superintendent Smith and Edward Bope, son of Colonel Bope, and counsel for the company, be compelled to come into court and testify as to their alleged conferences with McKinnis. Several days ago he had a subpoena issued for Edward Bope, but the sheriff is said to have been so far unable to serve it.

This is the second trial of the case, Mrs. Barnes having previously procured a verdict for $11,000, which was set aside by Judge Kinkade.

THANKSGIVING AT GRACE

Closing Event of a Day of Rejoicing for the Parish.

Helpful Sermon by the Rev. Dr. Brady and Informal Reception—Plans for Future.

The consecration of Grace Episcopal church by Bishop Leonard culminated...

MYRON H. LAMSON DEAD

Father of Members of Prominent Dry Goods Firm.

Long and Active Life—Assisted the Government During Civil War.

After a long and active life, Myron H. Lamson, father of the three members of the firm of Lamson Brothers, died yesterday afternoon at 4 o'clock at his late home, 123 West Woodruff avenue, aged eighty-four years. His was a life full of activity and usefulness that brought its reward in health and strength and only advanced age brought on the last illness.

He was born in Onondaga, N. Y., February 25, 1823, and spent his early life on a farm. He engaged in the trade of a watchmaker at Elbridge, N. Y., and during the second year of the civil war was engaged by the government at to Alexandria, Va., to become foreman of the building department of the gas works there. At the close of the war he returned to Elbridge and engaged in the manufacturing business and later went back to the farm. While foreman in the works at Alexandria, Mr. Lamson superintended the building of the presidential car for President Lincoln, but the first use to which the car was put was to carry the remains of the martyred President from Washington to Springfield.

In 1848 Mr. Lamson was married to Miss Laura Rhoades. Nineteen years ago, with their daughter, Miss Mary Lamson, they came to Toledo, where the three sons were engaged in the business that has made them so prominent in the city. Mrs. Lamson died May 1, 1892, and the daughter, Mary, and three sons, Julius M., J. E. B., and J. D. B. Lamson, survive him.

In his early life Mr. Lamson was a Whig in politics and later a Republican, and was president of the board in the village of Elbridge.

He was a member of the Baptist church in Elbridge and was coming to Toledo was identified with the Ashland Avenue Baptist church.

His funeral, which will be held Saturday afternoon at two o'clock, will take place from Ashland church, and remains will be placed in Woodlawn.

MAY HAVE A MURDERER

Police Arrest Hungarian in Railroad Yards.

Marshal at Woodburn, Ind., Was Killed Last Evening —Officers Coming.

In the arrest of John Pesnick, a Hungarian, whom Patrolman Minninger picked up in Oak Lake Shore yards at noon today the Toledo police have what may be one of the best captures of its kind made in some time. Pesnick is wanted at Woodburn, Ind., for the murder of the marshal of the place.

News of the murder of the marshal reached the police here in a mysterious manner. A woman with the stranger giving the name of...

435-437-439 Summit Street.

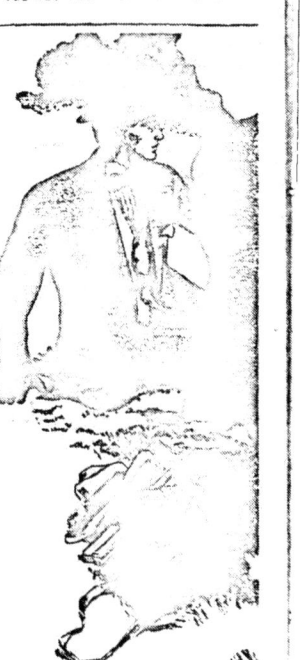

Copyright 1907 by Hart Schaffner

Clothes O[f]

THERE

MYRON H. LAMSON DEAD   (TOLEDO BLADE June 7, 1907)

FATHER of MEMBERS of PROMINENT
DRY GOODS FIRM

LONG and ACTIVE LIFE
ASSISTED GOVERNMENT DURING
CIVIL WAR

After a long and active life, Myron H. Lamson father of the three members of the firm of Lamason Brothers of Toledo, died yesterday afternoon at 3:45 o'clock at his late home, 122 West Woodruff Avenue, aged eighty-four years. His was a life full of activity and usefullness that brought its reward in health and strength and only advanced age brought on the last illness.

He was born in Onondaga, N.Y. February 25, 1823 and spent his early life on a farm. He engaged in the trade of wagonmaker at Elbridge, N.Y., and during the second year of the Civil War was engaged by the government to go to Alexandria, Virginia to become foreman of the building department of the car works there. At the close of the war he returned to Elbridge and engaged in the manufacturing business and later went back to the farm. While foreman in the works at Alexandria Mr. Lamason superintended the building of the presidential car for President Lincoln, but the first use to which the car was put was to carry the remains of the martyred President from Washington to Springfield, Illinois.

In 1848 Mr. Lamason was married to Miss Laura Rhoades. Nineteen years ago with their daughter, Miss Mary Lamason, they moved to Toledo, Ohio, where the three sons were engaged in the business that has made them so prominent in this city...The Lamason Brothers Company. Mrs. Lamason died May 1, 1892 and the daughter Mary and three sons Julius G., C.S.B. and J.D.R. Lamason survive him.

In his early life Mr. Lamason was a Whig in politics and later a Republican, and was president of the board in the Village of Elbridge.

NOT SO
HE WORKED
FOR THE
B & O

He was a member of the Baptist Church in Elbridge and since coming to Toledo was identified with the the Ashland Baptist Church.

His funeral, which will be held Saturday afternoon at 2 o'clock, will take place from Ashland church and the remains will be placed in Woodlawn.

Age.....84 Years

SEPTEMBER 1982
VOLUME XXI, NUMBER 5

FEATURES

14 — Inside A Beleagured City: Commander Prince John Magruder, By Mark Grimsley
Yorktown's general was an actor

18 — Inside A Beleagured City: The Siege Of Yorktown—Part II, By Charles F. Bryan, Jr.
Would it be the war's last battle?

30 — Inside A Beleagured City: Gallery
A camera's view of Yorktown

36 — Inventing The Future Face Of Warfare: Henry's Rifle, By Les Jensen
A history of the famous .44 repeater

38 — The Battle Of McDowell: Our Little Band Of Heroes, Edited by David Cornelius
"He could curse the Rebels to take better aim"

40 — Following The Flag For The Journal: The Career Of Carleton Coffin, By John Taylor
Covering four years of war on all fronts

Page 14

THE REGULARS

4 — Authors' Corps
6 — Behind The Lines
   By John E. Stanchak
7 — Mail Call
10 — Book Reviews
12 — The Gates Report
   By Arnold Gates
48 — The War In Words
   By James I. Robertson, Jr.

OUR COVER: From the collections of the Museum of the Confederacy, Richmond, Virginia, a McClellan model Confederate saddle used by Captain W. Stuart Symington and a .44 caliber Henry Rifle presented to Jefferson Davis' bodyguards on his 1865 flight from the Rebel capital.

ON THE BACK: A Federal 1st sargeant with his Henry repeater. From the collection of Herb Peck, Jr.

Page 29

Page 43

MAIL CALL

WHERE IS THE LINCOLN FUNERAL CAR?

Dear Editor,

In no way would I consider myself strictly an ardent Civil War Buff. But, do I ever enjoy the reading of every last word of each edition. First acquaintance was when a friend gave me a stack a foot high of old editions. I have no idea just how long I've been a subscriber. Never do I throw or give them away . . . just stack them up in the ol' attic . . . for reference reading.

My comprehension of the Civil War was way off base until I read the *Civil War Times*. And I am still learning.

I'm more of a Lincoln Buff. I receive *Lincoln Lore* from the Lincoln National Life. Also, for years I've subscribed to *Lincoln Herald* magazine. My room is jammed with Lincoln books. I'm crowding seventy-three and for sixty of those years my interest has been old Abe. I've traveled in his footsteps and learned an awful lot.

Back in 1968, while watching the Bobby Kennedy Funeral Train on TV the thought struck me, out of the blue, as to what had ever happened to the Abraham Lincoln Railroad Funeral Car? Being an avid Lincoln and railroad buff it aroused my curiosity. Since that day I have haunted the tracks of the historical old railroad vehicle. Today, you would have to see the vast accumulation of pictures and other related material to really appreciate it.

My memory tells me that once, somewhere, I saw an index of *Civil War Times* articles. There were a few on Lincoln but never one on the Lincoln Railroad Funeral Car.

Today, still searching but I'm sort of at the bottom of the barrel. Most of the basics have been covered and now I'm after the nitty-gritty, off beat info . . . the difficult stuff.

For instance, the Abraham Lincoln Car burned in a raging prairie grass fire at Columbia Heights out in Minneapolis on March 11, 1911. Pictures of its burning appeared in the Sunday, March 19, 1911 Minneapolis *Star*. I've a photocopy of the paper, but it is from microfilm.

As you well know, microfilm does not make for good quality pictures. I've racked my constitution in an effort to find an original copy, maybe the original photos, with little success. Maybe sometime, as I never give up.

Frankling B. Snow bought the car from the Union Pacific in 1904 and exhibited it at the St. Louis Exposition. I've a photo of it there. In 1905 Hon. Thomas Lowry paid off a mechanical lien on it and hauled it off to Minneapolis. He was the street car and real estate tycoon of that era in Minneapolis.

The original four trucks of the Lincoln Car were designed by a W.W. SNOW of the Union Tyre & Wheel Company of Jersey City. They made the trucks. The wheels were cast from exploded Civil War cannon in Wilmington.

There just has to be some connection between the two men. I'm doing genealogical research on the Snow family in Jersey City to see what is what.

That Union Tyre & Wheel Co. was the fore-runner of the Rampo Iron Works, railroad equipment manufacturers. I've a copy of the patent on the wheels. Soon as time is available I'll search for the truck patent.

Did you ever see the nine letters written by Secretary of War Stanton, Ward Lamons, Brevet Major General Meigs, a Mr. Robinson and McClure relative to the sale of the Lincoln Car to the Union Pacific Railroad in April of 1866? Makes revealing info. Josephine Cobb dug them out of the Bureau of Archives for me.

Originally it was just curiosity, but then I might write a book. But my best effort so far is a 150-slide presentation. Just never seem to get all the loose ends tied down when some new ones pop up.

As Mr. Hickey at the Illinois Museum states, it is not so much me that they consider but they do not want all of this info tossed into the garbage in case I cash in my chips. No worry, my wife will pass it on as per instructions.

Could some of your readers assist me in my efforts?

Frank W. Cornell
Lewiston, New York

CARRY ME BACK . . .

Dear Editor,

In the November 1981 issue I read with interest the review of Kenneth E. O[...] *Music and Muskets: Bands*

Continued on page 8

CLEAVES, FREEMAN:
MEADE OF GETTYSBURG

Perhaps the most reliable book on Meade, well documented and judicious - C. W. Books

$15.00

Plus U.P.S. Delivery Charge - $2.00
(Ohio Residents Add 6% Sales Tax)
Satisfaction Guaranteed, or Money Back.
Check/MoneyOrd./M.Chg./Visa/Am.Exp.

MORNINGSIDE BOOKSHOP
P. O. Box 1087, 260 Oak Street
Dayton, Ohio 45401
513/461-6736

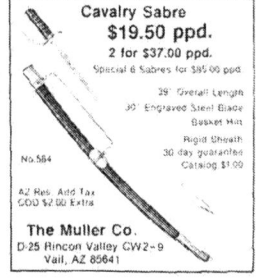

Cavalry Sabre
$19.50 ppd.
2 for $37.00 ppd.
Special 6 Sabres for $95.00 ppd

39" Overall Length
30" Engraved Steel Blade
Basket Hilt
Rigid Sheath
30 day guarantee
Catalog $1.00

No. 584

AZ Res. Add Tax
COD $2.00 Extra

The Muller Co.
D-25 Rincon Valley GW2-9
Vail, AZ 85641

THE MILITARY BOOKMAN

Military, Naval and Aviation History
Out-of-Print Books and Posters
29 East 93rd St., New York, NY 10028
212/348-1280

CIVIL WAR PHOTOGRAPHS
Buy • Sell • Trade

Largest Dealer in CDV's, Ambros, etc, Catlgs Avail. Free Appraisals; Americana Image Gallery, 88 Meade Dr. Gettysburg, PA 17325, 717-334-0751; WE BUY IMAGES

The 1983 Civil War Living History Calendar

Will be available November 1, 1982

- Little known CIVIL WAR Anecdotes and Facts
- Rare Photographs from the collection of the U.S. ARMY MILITARY HISTORY INSTITUTE
- Battle Dates and 1983 Re-enactments SHOOTS and LIVING HISTORY Exhibits

$8.00
(add 70¢ for postage)

P.O. Box 85, Preston, MD 21655
Send in 1983 EVENT DATES for FREE Publication!

LEE'S LAST CHANCE TO ESCAPE FROM PETERSBURG

CIVIL WAR
TIMES
APRIL 1995 — ILLUSTRATED

FAITHFUL FRIENDS
Army Dogs In The War

APPOMATTOX
Tour The Surrender Site

INFIGHTING AND BACKBITING
Officers, Yes. But Gentlemen?

A Rolling Memento

A splendid railroad coach was specially built to carry the president, but Lincoln never saw it. It carried only his corpse. Years later, it became a giant keepsake.

By DAVID K. NELSON

From August to October of 1858, Abraham Lincoln and Stephen A. Douglas held political debates throughout Illinois as they grappled for a seat in the U.S. House of Representatives. When the debate came to Galesburg on October 7, 15-year-old Thomas Lowry was among the eager spectators who crowded to hear the candidates' battle of words. Lowry admired Lincoln, and although history does not record it, there is a good chance he had an opportunity to speak with him that afternoon in Galesburg. The candidate had been his father's attorney for at least eight years, as evidenced by a still-extant letter from lawyer Lincoln to client Sam Lowry, dated August 17, 1850, concerning the title to some land Lowry wished to buy.

Young Thomas Lowry's family was sufficiently well-to-do to ensure that he was well educated. Three years after the debates, the intelligent, ambitious, and energetic young man entered Lombard University (since absorbed by Knox College) in Galesburg to study law. Lincoln was then just beginning his first term as U.S. president. Before Lowry finished his education, Lincoln was dead.

Lincoln's assassination was followed by one of the most elaborate state funerals in history. The president's body traveled in a special rail car from Washington, D.C., to Springfield, Illinois, for burial. Decades later, Lowry would purchase that rail car as a keepsake of his hero.

The railroad car that carried Lincoln in death had been designed to carry him in life. It was built at the U.S. Military

The car carrying Lincoln's body waits outside the train station in Harrisburg, the capital city of Pennsylvania. Here and in several other cities, the president's casket was removed from the train for public funeral services.

This memorial postcard, printed in 1908 by a Union veterans' organization, is based on a photo of the car taken after it was prepared for the funeral journey. The soldier standing on the steps at the far end is Myron Lamson, who oversaw the mechanical alterations to the car.

Railroad shops in the Orange and Alexandria Railroad yards in Alexandria, Virginia. B.P. Lamason, superintendent of car repair at those shops, designed the car as a mobile headquarters for Lincoln and his advisors.

Railroads of the time had a variety of track widths, or "gauges." To ensure that the presidential coach could travel anywhere rails were laid, Lamason specified "compromise" wheels, which had an unusually wide surface to accommodate the variety of gauges. The disadvantage of this wheel design was that it usually allowed the car to wander back and forth across the rails when the train was in motion, making for an uncomfortable ride. Lamason tried to ease this problem by fitting the car with 16 wheels — twice the usual number — and by paying careful attention to the car's weight and balance.

Although attempts to provide a smooth ride were probably not completely successful, every other effort was made to ensure the chief executive's comfort. The coach's walls were covered with tufted upholstery. Leather, velvet, and the intricate tassels associated with Victorian gentility abounded. But this was also a working vehicle, intended to be used for business. W.H.H. Price, the foreman who oversaw the car's construction, later recalled it "was divided into three compartments, viz., drawing-room, parlor and state room, the latter being the center of the car...."

Lincoln apparently had no urgent desire to take possession of his ornate coach. The records of the U.S. Military Railroad yard in Alexandria do not reflect any visit by the president to inspect the car after its completion. Certainly he never made any journey in the car before his assassination on April 15 of that year.

The timing and nature of Lincoln's death conspired to make his funeral one of the grandest events of its kind in American history. His body would be sent to Springfield on a special train. It would follow in reverse the same route President-elect Lincoln had traveled to reach Washington in 1861.

U.S. Military Railroad mechanic Sergeant Myron H. Lamson oversaw the transformation of the presidential passenger car into a presidential funeral car. He and his workers built a cata-

The car carrying Lincoln's body was not the only one festooned with black crepe. The entire train, including the often-changed locomotives and coal cars, wore mourning clothes. Here the train sits at Harrisburg, the station shown on the previous page, viewed from the other side.

The funeral car at the Orange and Alexandria rail yards shortly after its completion, but before modification for the funeral (above). It would see hard use; the photo at left shows it in Omaha, Nebraska, where it was displayed in 1898. The most visible change was the replacement of the four original trucks of "compromise" wheels with two standard-gauge wheel trucks.

falque inside the car to hold Lincoln's coffin. They removed the ornate brass railing from one end of the car and installed a roller to help load and unload the casket. While Lamson and his crew focused on functional alterations to the car, another group decorated it for the occasion. It was decked with black satin draping, silver fringe, and tassels.

During the funeral ride, Lincoln's body shared the car with a special honor guard and with the coffin of little Willie Lincoln, who had died on February 20, 1862. Willie had been enclosed in the family tomb of William Carroll, clerk of the Supreme Court, in Oak Hill Cemetery in Georgetown. It seemed appropriate that the son should go home to Illinois with his father, so his casket was disinterred for the trip.

Preceded by a special pilot engine to make sure the track was clear, the train left Washington at 8:00 A.M. on Friday, April 21, carrying friends and a large group of dignitaries. The president's eldest son, Robert, attended the departure, but it is uncertain whether he was a passenger. Some newspaper accounts of the time placed him on the train, but late in life he recalled traveling to meet the procession in Springfield rather than journeying with his father's body. Mary Todd Lincoln, the president's wife, was definitely not aboard; emotionally distraught, she elected not to make the trip.

With the exception of Cincinnati, Ohio, the train passed through every major city Lincoln had visited on his inaugural trip to Washington in 1861. In each city the coffin was removed and taken to some place of honor for funeral services. In all, the train made scheduled stops in 10 cities: Harrisburg and Philadelphia in Pennsylvania; New York, Albany, and Buffalo in New York; Cleveland and Columbus, Ohio; Indianapolis, Indiana; Chicago; and finally Springfield on May 3.

In Springfield the caskets were transferred to a special hearse imported from St. Louis, Missouri, for the purpose. The funeral cortege made its way by wagon, horseback, and foot to the interment ceremony. The railroad coach was then returned to the military shops at Alexandria, where it was an object of considerable public interest. It continued to be officially designated as the president's personal car, but there is no record that it was ever again used as such.

After the surrender of all Confederate forces, the U.S. War Department set about dismantling the apparatus of war. All military railroad equipment was eventually designated for disposal. One of Lincoln's closest friends, Ward Hill Lamon, purchased the funeral car in 1866 for $6,800. Lamon acted on behalf of T.C. Durant, who was then building the Union Pacific Railroad. Secretary of War Edwin Stanton was overseeing the demobilization of the Union military, and was concerned that the funeral car might become a sideshow exhibit, so Durant engaged Lamon to make the purchase to help allay Stanton's fears. Durant did not put the car on display; he used it as his personal car.

In 1874 the Union Pacific sold the car to the Colorado Central Railroad for $3,000. Its new owners stripped the car of its luxurious trappings and pressed it into everyday service. Eventually, however, the Union Pacific regained possession of the car and put it in storage in its shops.

At some time, one of the railroad companies that owned the car replaced the original 16-compromise-wheel carriage with a more conventional 8-wheel carriage. The compromise wheels where rendered unnecessary by the development of a nationwide standard gauge for railroad tracks. Interestingly, the Federal legislation that defined and encouraged the standard gauge had been supported and signed into law in the 1860s by Lincoln.

In 1898, the Union Pacific rail line displayed the funeral car at the Trans-Mississippi Centennial Exposition in Omaha, Nebraska, where more than a million people had an opportunity to see it. In 1904 it was sold to Franklyn Snow of Peoria, Illinois, who displayed it that same year at the St. Louis World's Fair. Contemporary newspaper accounts record that it was part of a special "Lincoln Museum" display that also included a log cabin alleged to be the one in which Lincoln was born. After the World's Fair ended, Snow, apparently in financial difficulties, offered the car for sale in 1905. It was then that Thomas Lowry heard it had survived.

At the age of 24, Lowry had left his family home at Pleasant View, Illinois, to seek his fortune in the fast-growing frontier town of Minneapolis, Minnesota. When he set up his law practice there, the town had 10,000 inhabitants; its oldest building had existed only 16 years. Lowry never truly found success as a lawyer, but he did thrive in business and eventually became famous as a prime mover in the development of what would become a sprawling metropolitan area.

Shortly after his arrival he made his first real investment in Minnesota: the purchase on promissory note of two building lots. While his fortunes went up and down with the changing national economy, at various times he owned or contracted for deeds to so much property that tracing his deals is a formidable task. If he had been able to hold onto every property he purchased, his descendants would now own roughly one third of the entire city of Minneapolis.

The Lincoln funeral car eventually became a museum piece. Partially restored, it was displayed at the 1904 World's Fair in St. Louis, Missouri (right). Thomas Lowry (left), a Minnesota land speculator and public-transportation mogul who had long idolized Lincoln, later bought it as a keepsake — and perhaps for its publicity value.

It is not for real estate speculation that modern residents of the Twin Cities remember Lowry, however. He is most noted as a founder of the area's original public transport system. Beginning with a permit for four miles of trackage right-of-way and a few horsedrawn coaches, he established scheduled passenger routes for shoppers and businessmen who wanted to get from place to place in town at a reasonable price.

Eventually, Lowry's modest venture expanded into a complex electrified streetcar network that covered virtually all of Minneapolis and St. Paul. So extensive was the system that it stretched from its eastern terminus at Stillwater, on the Wisconsin border, to Lake Minnetonka, west of Minneapolis. During the course of the mergers and stock offerings that financed the trolley's expansion, Lowry ceased to be the system's sole owner. But he grew wealthy in the process, wealthy enough by 1905 to buy a souvenir that nobody in the world could duplicate: the Lincoln funeral car.

Lowry transferred the car to Minneapolis, where he displayed it near some building lots he was trying to sell in the northern suburb of Columbia Heights. When the Grand Army of the Republic, the primary national organization for Union veterans, convened its 42d Encampment in Minneapolis in 1908, many of the veterans paid tribute to one of the last surviving relics directly associated with Lincoln.

Sometime between 1908 and 1911 the car was apparently sold or donated to the Columbia Heights Land Company, which Lowry had founded but in which he was only a part-owner. Lowry died in 1909, and his family claimed the car had been promised to the Minnesota Federation of Women's Clubs for preservation. There was some controversy over ownership of the car, but it was finally scheduled to be moved to Mendota, Minnesota, during the summer of 1911.

On March 18, 1911, a boy burning brush near the corner of Minneapolis's 35th Avenue N.E. and Architect Avenue lost control of his fire. The area, recently developed and still very rustic, had an abundance of prairie grass and fields in which residents grew crops. When the fire's flames, fanned by a stiff wind, ignited the dry prairie grass, the blaze quickly spread northward. Several other boys and neighborhood women who realized what was happening tried to control the fire. Their chief concern was to protect houses and barns; stopping the fire was already hopeless.

Most of the local men were away at work when the fire broke out, but Fire Chief Charles Amidon, assisted by former fireman W.D. Smith, formed the volunteers into bucket brigades to protect buildings. Battling with water-soaked brooms and blankets, the ad hoc squads managed to save most of the endangered structures, though virtually all the residents' crops were incinerated.

One area in which there was no possibility of controlling the fire was the Columbia Heights Land Company property at the corner of 37th and Quincy. Before the fire burned out, it consumed roughly 10 city blocks, including the land office and the Lincoln car. Auge Swanson, son of the postmaster, organized several boys in an attempt to save the coach. Ian McKnight, age 12, and Burdette Whitman, age 14, suffered burns during the struggle. The car was inside a shed, and by the time the fire-fighters realized the building was doomed, it was too late to rescue the relic. The shed was destroyed and the car damaged beyond repair.

As part of the considerable news coverage of the event, the March 19, 1911, Sunday *Tribune* and the *Journal* reported that the erstwhile manager of the land company, Edmund G. Walton, was permitting the public to take whatever souvenirs of the Lincoln car they could scrounge from the debris. Hundreds of people visited the site, and many carried away pieces of twisted metal and chunks of charred wood.

Several authentic mementos of the railroad car's destruction survived. The Lincoln College in Lincoln, Illinois, owns a piece of wood from the wreck. An article in the Minneapolis *Star* in March 1964 related that Maury Ostrander, then an associate professor at the University of Minnesota, had been a small boy at the time of the fire. He was still wearing a tie clasp he had made from a piece of window molding recovered from the ruin of the funeral car. No doubt dozens of other relics of the car are still kept in Minnesota homes, though few of the roughly two million current Twin Cities-area residents are familiar with the history and fate of the Lincoln car.

Tom Lowry's name, on the other hand, is still familiar there. A street in Minneapolis bears his name, and a statue of Lowry was dedicated in 1915. Interstate Route 94 now runs under the hill where his final house sat; this stretch of highway is called the Lowry Hill Tunnel. A lifelong admirer of Lincoln, Lowry wrote his own book of memories of the 16th president, which was published after the developer's death.

If Lowry's beloved souvenir has been forgotten, it will not long remain so. Illinois Benedictine College in Lisle, Illinois, has undertaken a project sure to return the Lincoln funeral train to the attention of historically minded Americans. Dr. Wayne Wesolowski, a chemistry professor at the college and an avid railroad modeler, is overseeing an effort to build a $1/12$-scale model of the funeral train to commemorate the 130th anniversary of the funeral this spring.

Included in the model are the funeral car itself, the locomotive *Nashville*, which pulled the train over much of its journey, Lincoln's coffin, and the special hearse which received the coffin on its arrival in Springfield. As *Civil War Times Illustrated* goes to press the coach and locomotive have been finished and the hearse and coffin models near completion. Dr. Wesolowski said the college hopes to send an exhibit, including the model train and photos of the original, on a tour that will include every major stop on the funeral train's route from Washington to Springfield. The exhibit's ability to visit cities outside the Midwest will depend on availability of funds. Volunteers from the National Model Railroad Association will help display the exhibit and provide information to visitors at each stop.

The railroad car that carried Lincoln's body was perhaps the ultimate expression of Victorian rail travel. In 1865 it captivated the attention of Americans of both North and South. Today, even at $1/12$ its original size, the car remains a powerful memento of the Civil War's most renowned martyr. Certainly it has earned distinction as one of the most evocative vehicles in American history. ■

Dr. Wayne Wesolowski and the $1/12$-scale model of the car, the construction of which he has overseen on behalf of Illinois Benedictine College. The college is seeking funds to send an exhibit, including this model, on tour to the cities the original car visited.

David Nelson is a professional technical writer who resides in Brooklyn Park, Minnesota.

CORINNE CAIN, LTD.
Fine Arts Appraiser / Art Consultant
326 West Harmont Drive
Phoenix, AZ 85021-5643 USA
(602) 279-2167
FAX (602) 906-0677

24 April 1996

Carolyn Texley
The Lincoln Museum
200 East Berry Street
Fort Wayne, Indiana   46801-7838

Dear Carolyn,

My latest conversation has been with Kim Bauer of the Illinois Historical Society. He is about to see what appears in their files.

The single panel that the Chicago Historical Society sounds like it could be a cousin to those belonging to Union Pacific as it features a little girl in pink with a basket on her arm within a round medallion shape outlined in gold, although I believe that they said their panel was painted grey.

Compare these to your panels and if you would, please send me xeroxes and physical descriptions of your panels for my files (to include dimensions of the panels please). The faxes were very difficult to read.

Meanwhile I feel sated. Having watched Murder One's finale, I finally know who killed Jessica Costello (nuts but true).

Best wishes and thank you for your help!!

Sincerely,

Corinne Cain

I will look forward to visiting your museum!

 Senior Member of American Society of Appraisers
Fine Arts & Native American Arts

#33
Artist   Unknown
Dates and Nationality
Medium   Oil on wood panel
Size   13 5/8" height X 13 5/8" width   (painted area)
                14 1/2" height X 15 1/4" width   (panel dimensions)
Signed   Not visible
Condition   Panel has been rejoined using epoxy two inches down from top edge. Chicago Conservation Center in November 1984 cleaned, retouched and applied a Soluvar varnish to each of the panels. Abrasions have been inpainted in an obvious manner.
Date   Circa 1865
Description   Pink flourishes have been painted at each corner. Inside 11 1/3" gold roundel is a landscape scene featuring a wooden bridge with two figures. Behind them is a large waterfall with trees on either side.
Provenance   Part of Lincoln's private railway car as decorative panels.

Fair Market Value

Created for him for his private railroad car, but as was completed in March or April 1965 Washington to Springfield was used to carry his body.

#34
Artist   Unknown
Dates and Nationality
Medium   Oil on wood panel
Size   14 5/8" height X 13 1/2" width   (painted area)
                  16 ¼" height X 15 1/2" width   (panel dimensions)
Signed   Not visible
Condition   Chicago Conservation Center in February 1985 cleaned, retouched
                  and applied a Soluvar varnish to each of the panels. Abrasions that
                  have been inpainted are obvious as no fill was added. Yellow varnish
                  staining is evident along the perimeter.
Date   Circa 1865
Description   French blue flourishes adorn each of the four corners. Within the gold
                  roundel that measures 11 1/3" in diameter is a female figure with
                  large white wings whose right hand rests on a round portrait of George
                  Washington. She is carrying a plant sprig in her left hand.
Provenance   Part of Lincoln's private railway car as decorative panels.

Fair Market Value

Created for him for his private railroad car, but as was completed in March or April 1965
Washington to Springfield was used to carry his body.

#35
Artist	Unknown
Dates and Nationality
Medium	Oil on wood panel
Size	14 1/2" height X 13 1/2" width	(painted area)
	16" height X 15 1/4" width	(panel dimensions)
Signed	Not visible
Condition	Chicago Conservation Center in February 1985 cleaned, retouched and applied a Soluvar varnish to each of the panels. Retouching is evident as infill was not added first. Staining from old varnish is somewhat visible along perimeter of painted area.
Date	Circa 1865
Description	Pink flourishes have been painted at each corner. Inside roundel that is defined by a gold band is an outdoor scene with a still brook in the foreground Flowering plants are in bloom along the back edge of the water. Mountains are in the distance after thick areas of trees.
Provenance	Part of Lincoln's private railway car as decorative panels.

Fair Market Value

Created for him for his private railroad car, but as was completed in March or April 1965 Washington to Springfield was used to carry his body.

#36
Artist   Unknown
Dates and Nationality
Medium   Oil on wood panel
Size   14 5/8" height X 13 5/8" width   (painted area)
                16" height X 15 1/4" width   (panel dimensions)
Signed   Not visible
Condition   Chicago Conservation Center in November 1984 cleaned, retouched
                and applied a Soluvar varnish to each of the panels. Retouching is
                obvious as no infill was added first. Faint stains from old varnish
                remain visible.
Description   Pink painted flourishes adorn each of the four corners. Inside the
                11 1/3" gold ringed roundel is a seascape featuring a sailboat with
                a single sail raised immediately in front of a light house. There is
                a large ship on the horizon line.
Provenance   Part of Lincoln's private railway car as decorative panels.

Fair Market Value

Created for him for his private railroad car, but as was completed in March or April 1965
Washington to Springfield was used to carry his body.

#37
Artist Unknown
Dates and Nationality
Medium Oil on wood panel
Size 14 5/8" height X 13 1/2" width   (painted area)
  16" height X 15 1/4" width   (panel dimensions)
Signed Not visible
Condition Chicago Conservation Center in November 1984 cleaned, retouched and applied a Soluvar varnish to each of the panels. Retouching is noticeable as infill was not added first. Faint evidence of varnish staining is around perimeter of painted portion. The panel is cracking from the left side measuring 2 ½".
Date Circa 1865
Description Pink flourishes were painted at each of four corners. Within 11 1/3" roundel is an outdoor scene depicting a woman walking away from the viewer. There is a two story building at viewer's right. Three sailboats are on the lake at midground. There is a large boulder in the immediate foreground.
Provenance Part of Lincoln's private railway car as decorative panels.

Fair Market Value

Created for him for his private railroad car, but as was completed in March or April 1965 Washington to Springfield was used to carry his body.

#38
Artist	Unknown
Dates and Nationality	
Medium	Oil on wood panel
Size	14 5/8" height X 13 1/2" width (painted area)
	16" height X 15 1/4" width (panel dimensions)
Signed	Not visible
Condition	Chicago Conservation Center in February 1985 cleaned, retouched and applied a Soluvar varnish to each of the panels. Retouching is noticeable as infill was not used. Faint staining from old varnish is evident along perimeter.
Date	Circa 1865
Description	Pink flourishes are painted at each corner. Within the 11 1/3" in diameter roundel is an outdoor scene that reveals a woods clearing in the foreground. A large lake separates the clearing from many buildings on the other side of the lake backed by pale blue mountains.
Frame	
Provenance	Part of Lincoln's private railway car as decorative panels.

Fair Market Value

Created for him for his private railroad car, but as was completed in March or April 1965 Washington to Springfield was used to carry his body.

#39
Artist   **Unknown**
Dates and Nationality
Medium   Oil on wood panel
Size   14 5/8" height X 13 1/2" width   (painted area)
                16 1/2" height X 15 1/4" width   (panel dimensions)
Signed   Not visible
Condition   Chicago Conservation Center in February 1985 cleaned, retouched
                and applied a Soluvar varnish to each of the panels. Retouching is
                distinguishable as infill was not used. Panel is cracking horizontally.
                From the viewer's left side the crack measures 2 ½". From the viewer's
                right side the crack measures 2" in length. Faint yellow staining is
                visible around perimeter of painted area.
Date   Circa 1865
Description   French blue flourishes are painted on each of the four corners. Within
                the 11 1/3" in diameter roundel outlined in gold metallic paint is a
                single figure wearing a yellow drum with red rims. He holds two sticks
                as though playing the drum while he glances toward the viewer's left.
                There is a wood enclosure at left foreground. The drummer is wearing
                a blue coat with gold buttons. His hat has a red feather attached in front.
Provenance   Part of Lincoln's private railway car as decorative panels.

Fair Market Value

Created for him for his private railroad car, but as was completed in March or April 1965
Washington to Springfield was used to carry his body.

#32
Artist			Unknown
Dates and Nationality
Medium			Oil on wood panel
Size			14 3/4" height X 14 3/4" width			(painted area)
			16" height X 15 1/4" width			(panel dimensions)
Signed			Not visible
Condition		Chicago Conservation Center in November 1984 cleaned, retouched
			and applied a Soluvar varnish to each of the panels. Retouching is
			particularly evident just below the roundel's bottom edge. Craquelure
			was present before conservation undertaken remains visible, but appears
			to be stable. Evidence of yellowing varnish along outside edges of
			composition.
Date			Circa 1865
Description		French blue flourishes are painted at each corner. Gold encircled roundel
			measures 11 1/3" in diameter. It contains a scene with a ship at sail
			perilously close to rocky shore in an active sea.
Provenance		Part of Lincoln's private railway car as decorative panels.

Fair Market Value

Created for him for his private railroad car, but as was completed in March or April 1965 Washington to Springfield was used to carry his body.

#31
Artist   Unknown
Dates and Nationality
Medium   Oil on wood panel
Size   9" height X 3 1/3" width   (painted area)
                 10" height X 7 ½" width   (panel dimensions)
Signed   Not visible
Condition   Fair to good. Craquelure is severe. Lifting of pigment has taken
                 place at very bottom. There is a ¼" abrasion above the roundel.
Date   Circa 1865
Description   An eagle with its wings outstretched has a red ribbon winding above
                 and below the bird. There are boats in the background on either
                 side of the bird. Grey and dark tan lines drawn above and below
                 the roundel serve to visually contain the composition like a
                 decorative border.
Provenance   Part of Lincoln's private railway car as decorative panels.

Fair Market Value

Created for him for his private railroad car, but as was completed in March or April 1965 Washington to Springfield was used to carry his body.

This one decorated a panel near a clerestory window

Panel from the Lincoln Funeral Car held by the Lincoln Financial Foundation Collection

Panel from the Lincoln Funeral Car held by the Lincoln Financial Foundation Collection

9 January 1996

Dear Mr. Prokopowsich,

Enclosed you will find a copy of an article from *Locomotive Engineering* dated September 1893. It was written by my great-grandfather, William Henry Harrison Price.

The other enclosure is the piece I wrote about my great-grandfather from what I was able to verify from my research. I have been able, since writing the article, to determine that they did, in fact, live in Mt. Vernon, Illinois. This was verified on a trip to the genealogy department of the Mt. Vernon library in an old city directory. I am sure W.H.H. was employed at the big railroad car building shop that existed there for many years.

Sorry it took so long to get this to you. Holidays, travelling and snow seemed to have gotten in the way.

It was a pleasure meeting you at the Newburgh library last November. I enjoyed your talk very much.

Sincerely,

Margaret A. (Price) Lant

FREDERIC REMINGTON

Buffalo Runners, Big Horn Basin
1909, oil on canvas, 30 1/8" x 51 1/8".
Courtesy Sid Richardson Collection of Western Art, Fort Worth, Texas.

it connected directly to the train-pipe instead of the main drum. The chances are that the governor connection with the old valve was made with a tee on the train-pipe, and this was not changed when the new valve was put on.

With Mr. Lee, in his desire to have air-brakes taken care of, I heartily sympathize. There are altogether too many brakes in the country in a useless condition. By all means let us try to find some good systematic way of taking care of them. It seems to me the trouble is the proper one to make the repair, and if he were furnished with printed slips or blanks, he would be much more apt to get the facts down in intelligent shape.

Chicago, Ill.   PAUL SYNNESTVEDT

The Private Car Built for President Lincoln, 1863-1865.

Editors:

From time to time since 1866 the writer has noticed in the press and railway journals different articles in regard to the car which was built during the war for the private use of President Lincoln, and, as this important relic (now the property of the Union Pacific Railway Co.) is likely to attract considerable interest among the exhibits at Chicago, he undertakes to state for the benefit of the reading public what he knows of its history. It may be added, without impropriety, that there is probably no one now living more conversant with this matter than the writer, as will be shown before he is through.

Soon after the beginning of the war the old railroad shops at Alexandria, Va., were enlarged by the Government for the purpose of building and repairing cars. The work was under the immediate supervision of Mr. B. P. Lamason, superintendent in charge of all car work in Virginia, and the writer was one of his foremen.

Some time during the year 1863 Superintendent Lamason either conceived the idea or had received instructions to build a private car for the use of the President. The work was begun in November of that year, and was completed in February,

plates with curved slots, one on each track. There were eight side bearings made of spring steel and rubber.

The spread of trucks was 4 feet 10 inches, wheels, 33 inches, cast iron with broad tread. The springs in truck bolsters were hung on obstacle long hangers, no sandboard, but bottom of hangers tied with "U"-shaped under-rods.

No equalizing bar was used, the elliptic springs being placed on top of oil boxes. The pedestals were cast iron of a pattern so elaborate as to be difficult to describe, Mr. Lamason having spent weeks in designing them.

The outside of car was painted a rich chocolate brown, and polished with oil and rotten stone with the bare hand. In the oval center, on side of car, was painted the United States coat-of-arms, and in center of panel above the coat-of-arms, in small gold letters placed in a circle, were the words, "United States." Car was orna-

PRIVATE CAR BUILT FOR PRESIDENT LINCOLN IN 1864.

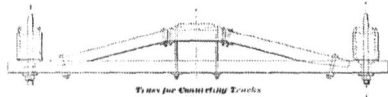

Trucks for Converting Tracks

A Defective Engineer's-Valve.

Editors:

We have the '92 engineer's brake-valve, with feed-valve attachment, on all engines here.

On one engine we have a valve which has caused considerable talk. The brake-valve handle can be moved to position for service application until the air is heard escaping from preliminary exhaust port from brake-valve reservoir, but not from the equalizing exhaust port, as it should; but, nevertheless, the tank and driver-brakes will be slowly applied, when engine is uncoupled from train.

Upon examination the rotary-valve was found to be in good condition, also the seat, packing good in equalizing discharge-valve piston, gaskets in good condition, and there are no flaws in castings, train-line not leaking. For a pointer, will say that rotary-valve is perforated, i. e., it is drilled

was coupled between the engine and train the stop-cock on the whistle-pipe at the rear of the train may have been open, or the whistle-valve on the engine may have worked a little hard and the air discharge-valves been partly choked up with cinders. The air-cock on the gauge "combination" having a larger opening, would reduce the pressure enough to blow the whistle all right.   M. E. WATTS.

West Nanticoke, Pa.

THE ANSWER

Editors:

The whistle-signal problem which I gave to the readers of LOCOMOTIVE ENGINEERING last month may be thus explained: There was a crack in rubber diaphragm close to the joint between chambers A and B and directly under port d. Now, my theory as to why the whistle would blow by opening small air-cock at the end of last coach and refused to blow when the conductor's valve was opened, is this: By opening conductor's valve, a considerable amount of air being discharged from whistle-pipe, the pressure in chamber B, instead of raising diaphragm, would rush through the crack in diaphragm to chamber A. Then port d, being so small, would check the flow of air enough to retain a pressure in chamber A sufficient to hold diaphragm down and prevent air escaping through seat and enough to blow the whistle; but the hole through the small air-cock, being but a very little larger than port d, would allow but a moderate amount of air to escape, or enough so that the pressure in chamber B would raise the diaphragm before it could force itself through the crack into chamber A and equalize. I have had several cases of this kind, and in every instance it was caused by the rubber diaphragm cracking near the joint.

Syracuse, N. Y.   W. F. RIVARD.

Conger's Pump-Governor.

Editors:

I had a governor that acted like Conger's, and after a great deal of trouble

William Henry Harrison Price
and
The Lincoln Funeral Car

Several years ago my uncle, Charles Price, of Mobile, Alabama, asked me if I still had the bowl that had been presented to my great-grandfather, William Henry Harrison Price, whom I will refer to henceforth as W.H.H. At the time he asked, I had no idea what bowl he was referring to. He explained that the bowl had been presented to W.H.H. in connection with his being the foreman in charge of building a railroad car for President Abraham Lincoln. Somewhere, in the far reaches of my mind, I did recall this great-grandfather being mentioned in connection with the Lincoln car, but hadn't paid much attention to the discussion. How I wish I had listened and asked questions, but I was just a small child then.

In 1990 I retired and one of my first projects was to get the many photographs I had collected into some semblance of order. Many of them came from my grandparents attic. I became interested in these old pictures and the people in them. This led me down the path of genealogy and what I can tell you about W.H.H. Price.

There were numerous things in my possession that meant nothing to me at the time, but now mean a great deal. I began gathering bits and pieces from several sources. Much was learned from the old family Bible given to Lydia in 1887 by her husband, W.H.H. Someone had carefully recorded births, marriages, and deaths. Information also came from an eighty-five year old man in Bowling Green, Indiana who has an interest in genealogy. And from my cousin, Charles McCoy Dugger of Miami, Florida, who has a wonderful mind that has retained a great deal of family information. He has been a constant source of help and encouragement to me.

William Henry Harrison Price was born on the 16th of November 1840 in Elizabethtown, Pennsylvania. He was the firstborn of Daniel and Catherine Jane (Sproat) Price. He had four brothers and four sisters. When he was about eleven years old, the family lived in Harrisburg, Pennsylvania, but for a number of years after that, I have been unable to determine where they lived until 1866. At that time, the family moved to the tiny town of Bowling Green, Indiana near Terre Haute. W.H.H. was twenty-six years old at that time and may not have moved there with them.

He had taken his apprenticeship in the trade of railroad car building at the Renova Pennsylvania Railroad Shop. According to his obituary he was considered one of the most expert car builders of the country. He was frequently mentioned in the trade journals in connection with his work. Other than his apprenticeship, it is not known where he was educated. However, it is evident that he was a very articulate man from reading his article.

When the Civil War began, he enlisted in the Union Army, but served only a short time. He accepted a position as a foreman at the United States Military Car Shop at Alexandria, Virginia. This probably occurred about 1862. In 1863 he was instructed to build a railroad car for President Lincoln. He served as the foreman of this project under the supervision of Colonel D.C. McCallum who was, according to an account about the car, an acting brigadier general who was the officer in charge of the Union Army's railroad system. Mr. B.P. Lamason was the superintendent of the shop and designer of the car.

At Christmas that year, W.H.H. was presented with a silver-plated bowl with a small medallion on it with an inscription that reads, "Presented to W.H.H.P. by the Employers of U.S.M.R.R. Dec. 25, 1863". This was the bowl my uncle had asked about and I found several years later while looking through things taken from my grandparents attic and stored by me for some eight to ten years.

The car was completed in February 1865 according to W.H.H. in an article he wrote for a publication of *Locomotive Engineering* dated September 1893. This article is one of my treasures as I have the original publication.

It is a well known fact that Lincoln never used the car while alive and family legend has it that he thought the car was far too pretentious for him. A considerable amount of information is available about the funeral car and the journey carrying the President from Washington to Springfield, Illinois. I remember the family talking about having pieces of the crepe that decorated the car and having seen it as a child. My mother told of my younger brother taking it to school for "show and tell". However, I did not find it among the things from the attic. I related this to my cousin, Charles Dugger, and said how sorry I was that I didn't know what had become of it. Several months went by, and one day in February 1994, a package arrived from Florida. To my surprise my cousin had sent me pieces of crepe, fringe, and silk cord taken from the car. W.H.H. confessed to having taken some of it in the article in *Locomotive Engineering*. We believe that small pieces of the decoration were given to various family members for keepsakes. The pieces he sent had belonged to his mother, Irene Price Dugger.

I asked Charles if he had anything else he would like to add. He stated he had no other information about the Lincoln car and that most of what he knew was from things our uncle Charlie and I had sent to him. He did tell me about locating the decorations. This is what he said: "I've got a little old trunk that used to be my grandfathers, my grandpa Dugger. There is a lot of little old stuff stuck in there, odds and ends, a few pictures. Nothing of any interest. Most all of the family pictures were lost when my parents moved to Rio de Janeiro and the ship carrying their personal items sunk. I found an envelope that has some of that Lincoln crepe and I want to be sure to send that to you. I don't have any use for it and I know that you would like to have it. There is not a whole lot left because everyone seemed to steal a little of it. I think I recall now that the kids took it to school and the teacher snipped off some of it. But there is enough there and I will send it on to you". I am thankful these items had not been destroyed and grateful to my cousin for giving them to me.

Now, back to W.H.H.. It was on the 13th of October, 1868 that W.H.H. was married to Lydia Ann de Hart in Nashville, Tennessee by Reverend D. Rutlege. A year later a son was born to them. He was William de Hart Price, my beloved grandfather whom I called Papa Bill. Two more sons followed, Samuel Kees Price and Jesse Shefield Price.

It is unclear where the family lived while raising these children, but I have reason to believe they may have spent some time in Mt. Vernon, Illinois. There was a large car shop there and it is quite possible W.H.H. may have been employed there. Part of my reasoning for this stems from the following: My aunt, Grace Price Biedelman, who will be 95 years old on July 25th, is one of my sources of information. When I visit with her I ask her to tell me anything she can remember about the family. She related to me recently that her father, William de Hart Price, was sent to Evansville to work from Mt. Vernon, Illinois.

While working here, her father met Parthenia Rose at an ice cream social. They were married and had seven children. My father, Conrad William Price, was their firstborn. They remained in Evansville the rest of their lives.

Samuel Kees Price also married in Evansville and lived here until his death. However, the third son, Jesse Shefield Price, was only fourteen years old when his parents moved to Georgia. Although he married in Salisbury, North Carolina, he lived in Atlanta for many years and died there.

According to the obituary of W.H.H., he moved from Evansville to Oakland City, Georgia in 1888 to take charge of the car repairing department of the Southern shop. Oakland City was about four miles outside Atlanta, near Ft. McPherson. Today, it is part of Atlanta. While there he was a member of the Knights of Honor, Dixon Lodge #569. He died there on the 8th of October 1898 at the age of 58, and was buried in Atlanta. His wife, Lydia, survived him until 1926. She took care of her mother, Elizabeth Osborne de Hart, who lived to be 105. I remember hearing a great deal more about Grandma de Hart and her age than I heard about W.H.H. and his accomplishments.

Learning about the replica of the funeral car being built by the Illinois Benedictine College was quite by accident. I'm grateful to Bill Bartelt for telling me of the project. I am really looking forward to seeing it next year when it tours.

It is a privilege to share these bits of information about the great-grandfather that I never knew, but who has become a very real person to me these last few years. I'm very proud to have been a part of his family.

This has been prepared and recorded by Margaret Anne Price Lant, Evansville, Indiana.
Dated: April 25, 1994

Margaret Anne Price Lant

Bibliography

1. Family Bible belonging to Lydia de Hart Price.

2. James E. Campbell - Records of Clay County, Indiana and The Old Settlers Methodist Church.

3. Charles McCoy Dugger, Miami, Florida, 1st cousin.

4. Grace Biedelman, Evansville, Indiana, aunt.

5. Obituary of William Henry Harrison Price. Atlanta newspaper.

6. Obituary of Charles Herr Price, Terre Haute, Indiana newspaper.

7. *The Atlanta Journal* - July 20, 1919, page 8.

8. *Locomotive Engineering*, September 1893, page 415.

9. Article "President Lincoln's Private Car".

10. "The Lincoln Funeral Car" - *Lincoln Lore* - Bulletin of the Lincoln National Life Insurance Company, Ft. Wayne, Indiana, Number 1431, May 1957.

http://www.orlandosentinel.com/news/local/southwest/orl-oc07jan17,0,6349152.story?coll=orl-news-headlines-swest

On the auction block

Everything including the sink Antiques at a Haines City auction aren't just family heirlooms. They have history.

Linda Florea
Sentinel Staff Writer

January 17, 2007

HAINES CITY -- What do Abraham Lincoln's sink, Japanese war propaganda and a square grand piano have in common? They will all be up for grabs Saturday at the House of David auction.

"It's going to have a lot of nice pieces that are going to be hard to find anywhere else," auctioneer Paul Hirneisen said. "It's something dealers would be interested in because of the variety of items as well as a good amount of collectibles and antiques."

One of the most unusual items in the auction will be a silver and brass folding lavatory sink that Hirneisen thinks was in a Pullman railroad car made for Abraham Lincoln in 1864. Although Lincoln never rode in the car, describing it as too fancy, it carried his body to Illinois for burial.

In 1929 the car was refitted and the sink was removed and purchased by a railroad worker. The worker passed on the sink to his son, who turned it over to Hirneisen to sell.

Although the Pullman company records were destroyed in a fire and the owner's original receipt was ruined in a flood, Hirneisen does have a statement from the buyer as to its authenticity.

"It's never been up for auction," Hirneisen said. "Our stance is family history, even verbal history, is a good background as long as everything fits into the right slot. If it didn't match up, it would be a different story."

Although the records are gone, the history of the railroad car the folding sink is said to have come from is at pullman-car.com/history/History.html. Hirneisen said he has researched the sink and is very certain it was taken from Lincoln's railroad car. The minimum starting bid will be $5,000.

Also on the auction block is a set of 34 Japanese propaganda prints, including one showing the landing on the Aleutian Islands in Alaska and another depicting Japanese bombers in formation over New York City. The prints are in the original case with a cover piece of rice paper explaining the scene in Japanese.

"The prints came from a man in the Pacific theater in World War II," Hirneisen said. "He got those in Japan as the war was ending."

Hirneisen said most of the Japanese propaganda was destroyed after Japan surrendered.

Another gem at the auction is a Victorian square parlor piano that came from Winter Haven. The ornate and rare piano is worth about $10,000 in its current condition, he said. In restored condition it would be worth $25,000 or more. The starting bid is $3,000.

While Haines City might not be the epicenter for antiquing, Hirneisen, who has run the auction in Haines City for more than nine years, said he sees a change in the way families handle their heirlooms.

"A lot of retirees come to this area, and what's happening is there is a change in the trend," he said. "You used to hand stuff down to the children. What we have found is most children do not want what the parents had -- most of the time they're interested in the money, not the memories."

He added that some retirees see their heirlooms as a retirement fund and are afraid their children will not know their true value.

House of David has auctions the first and third Saturday of the month and a coin auction once a month. Because of the unique pieces in Saturday's auction, instead of the usual 800 to 1,300 items from the estate auctions, there will be only about 400 items and about 60 or 70 antiques.

The preview begins at 9 a.m., The auction kicks off at 10. Prospective bidders may go to houseofdavidauctions.com for a look at the items and directions.

Bidders may place bids by phone and should call 863-412-4185 and leave basic information. When the item comes up for bid, an employee will call the bidder, although Hirneisen warns that there is no guarantee on the condition of any of the items sold over the phone.

Linda Florea can be reached at lflorea@orlandosentinel.comor 407-931-5951.

Copyright © 2007, Orlando Sentinel | Get home delivery - up to 50% off

www.ingramcontent.com/pod-product-compliance
Ingram Content Group UK Ltd.
Pitfield, Milton Keynes, MK11 3LW, UK
UKHW020209260325
456733UK00006B/35